Acclaim for MOISE

GROSS INDECENCY

NAMED ONE OF THE BEST PLAYS OF THE YEAR BY *Time, Newsday, The New York Post, The Advocate* AND *The New York Times.*

"A dazzling and thought-provoking piece, with a wit and ingenuity that are specifically of the theater."
—*Wall Street Journal*

"A triumph . . . truth, purity, and simplicity suffuse [this] thoroughly engrossing new play . . . sweeps away cobwebs and distortions, allowing complex, credible human beings to emerge from history." —*Time Out New York*

"A runaway hit." —*Washington Post*

"Amazing . . . a work of tremendous theatricality, passion, and compassion." —*New York Law Journal*

"Mr. Kaufman has created a work as artificial and mannered as a Wildean epigram. Yet within minutes of the first scene you have accepted its terms; you have already learned to think, in other words, in the original theatrical language that Mr. Kaufman has devised." —*New York Times*

"One of the most riveting and *theatrical* pieces of theater currently on the boards." —*Daily Variety*

MOISES KAUFMAN

GROSS INDECENCY

Moisés Kaufman is the founder and artistic director of Tectonic Theater Project, a theater company based in New York City. With Tectonic he has directed works by Samuel Beckett, Tennessee Williams, Benjamin Britten, Sophie Treadwell, and Christopher Ashley, as well as new works by Peter Golub and Naomi Iizuka. His direction of Franz Xaver Kroetz's *The Nest* was named one of the ten best productions of the 1994–95 season by the *Village Voice*. In 1993, a retrospective of his work was presented at the Consulate General of Venezuela in New York. He is the recipient of the 1997 Joe A. Callaway Award for excellence in the craft of stage direction given by the Stage Directors and Choreographers Foundation for his work on *Gross Indecency*.

Mr. Kaufman also directs regularly with Working Classroom, a multi-ethnic arts program that produces original plays written and performed by residents of Albuquerque, New Mexico. He has toured with this group throughout the U.S. and abroad.

In his native Venezuela, Mr. Kaufman performed as an actor with the Thespis Theater Ensemble, one of the country's foremost experimental theater companies. He has lived in New York City since 1987.

GROSS INDECENCY

The Three Trials of Oscar Wilde

MOISES KAUFMAN

VINTAGE BOOKS

A DIVISION OF RANDOM HOUSE, INC.

NEW YORK

A VINTAGE ORIGINAL, FEBRUARY 1998
FIRST EDITION

Library of Congress Cataloging-in-Publication Data
Kaufman, Moisés.
Gross indecency : the three trials of Oscar Wilde / Moisés Kaufman.
p.   cm.
"A Vintage original."
ISBN 0-375-70232-6
1. Wilde, Oscar, 1854–1900—Drama.   I. Title.
PR9333.9.K38G76   1997
812—dc21   97-37596
CIP

www.randomhouse.com

Printed in the United States of America
10 9 8 7 6 5 4

To Jeff LaHoste
without whom beauty would be impossible.

CONTENTS

ix

ACKNOWLEDGMENTS

It took me two years to write *Gross Indecency*. During this time, many people contributed to the development of this work. I am especially grateful to:

The many actors who participated in workshops and staged readings of *Gross Indecency*. They helped shape this play.

The exceptional team of actors, designers, and stage manager whose names are listed in this edition. They shared with me a sense of wonder that was necessary to the creation of this work. They inspired me to do my best work both as a writer and a director.

Steve Wangh, who told me I had to write this play and then helped me do it. He is a master teacher and a friend.

Jim Nicola and the staff of New York Theatre Workshop, who have been keen supporters of this play from its inception.

Bernard Gersten, who came into our lives at a decisive moment. His guidance and support changed the destiny of this play.

Peter Cane, Joyce Ketay, Kevin McAnarney, Chase Mishkin, Leonard Soloway, Steven Levy, Alan Schuster, and Barbara Eliran, who were instrumental in the success of this play's commercial run. I could not have done it without them.

Larry Kramer, whose advice was always right on target.

Nan Elsasser, Arthur Bartow, Joe and Jeanne Sullivan, and the New York State Council for the Arts, who are among Tectonic Theater Project's strongest supporters. Their faith in us and their grace made the writing of this play possible.

Fernando Ivosky and the Thespis Theater Ensemble, who taught me what theater can do. They will always have a place in my heart.

Dora, José, Ariel, Esther, Perla, Ezri, Andrea, and, more recently, Valerie, who have been my life support system.

Special thanks to Merlin Holland and The Estate of Oscar Wilde for permission to reprint extracts from *De Profundis* and from Wilde's letters still in copyright.

Finally, I want to thank everyone who has worked with us at Tectonic Theater Project over these past five years. This is for you!

AUTHOR'S INTRODUCTION

Three years ago a friend gave me a book entitled *The Wit and Humor of Oscar Wilde*, which contained a collection of his epigrams and witticisms. It was amusing and clever and presented a biting satire of Victorian mores—the sort of thing I had come to expect from Oscar Wilde.

The last ten pages of the book, however, were transcripts of Wilde's trials. In these pages I found a fascinating event: an artist being asked to justify his art in a court of law! Wilde's responses about the nature and purpose of art surprised me. I recognized in them a purity and clarity of thought I had not encountered before.

This led me to re-read his plays and theoretical writings. I was intrigued by his attention to form, his passion for language, and his belief in the possibilities of art.

I think this struck a chord with me because questions about language and form have fascinated me since I became involved in the theater. How does theater communicate? What constitutes a theatrical vocabulary? How can we redefine our theatrical language as our understanding of knowledge and communication changes?

In my teens I attended the International Theater Festival in my native city of Caracas, Venezuela. There I saw Grotowsky's Laboratory Theater performing *Acropolis*; Tadeusz Kantor's Cricot Theater performing *The Dead Class*; Peter Brook's company performing *Ubu Roi*; and Pina Bausch with the Wuppertal Tanz Theater. Later, I was to see Richard Foreman's work. These were my earliest experiences in the theater. They were thrilling, original, and inspiring.

These pieces did not imitate reality but, rather, created a separate reality on the stage—a reality that followed only its own internal logic. The performance style, the body language of the actors, their vocal techniques, the treatment of the theatrical space, each of these elements had been developed and combined to create a new world on the stage—a new world that could exist *only* on a stage.

When I founded Tectonic Theater Project, I dedicated myself and the company to producing works that explore theatrical language and form. For the past five years, this has been the focus of my work as both a writer and director.

In making *Gross Indecency: The Three Trials of Oscar Wilde* I was interested in two things: First, I wanted to tell the story— *a* story—of these trials. And second, I was interested in using this story to continue to explore theatrical language and form. Specifically, how can theater reconstruct history?

Very early in the process of researching the play, I found that there were as many versions of what had occurred at the trials as there were people involved. George Bernard Shaw, Lord Alfred Douglas, Frank Harris, Oscar Wilde, each told a very personal, sometimes very different, story of what happened.

It seemed to me that any legitimate attempt to reconstruct this historical event had to incorporate, in one way or another, the diversity of accounts. This posed a fascinating problem: how to create a theater piece that could encompass all the different stories, and yet have a coherent, dramatic through-line.

As director, I saw that such a reconstruction also posed a number of questions. As soon as the actors began to personify historical characters, they brought to these portrayals their own histories, their own "versions" of who the characters were and what the conflict between them was about. I knew that the piece had to make that presence—the presence of the actor telling the story—visible.

The play you are about to read is an attempt to deal with these questions.

GROSS INDECENCY

"The truth is rarely pure and never simple."
—*Oscar Wilde*

.

Gross Indecency: The Three Trials of Oscar Wilde was written by
Moisés Kaufman. The dramaturg was Stephen Wangh. It was
first produced on the stage by Tectonic Theater Project at the
Greenwich House Theatre in New York City on February 27,
1997. It was directed by Moisés Kaufman; the set design was by
Sarah Lambert; costume design by Kitty Leech; lighting design by Betsy Adams; sound design/score by Wayne Frost; and
the stage manager was Rachel Putnam. The cast was as follows:

OSCAR WILDE	Michael Emerson
LORD ALFRED DOUGLAS, NARRATOR 7	Bill Dawes
QUEENSBERRY, GILL, LOCKWOOD, NARRATOR 8	Robert Blumenfeld
CLARKE, OTHERS, NARRATOR 6	Trevor Anthony
CARSON, NARRATOR 5	John McAdams
NARRATOR 1, WOOD, SHAW, OTHERS	Greg Pierotti
NARRATOR 2, ATKINS, WRIGHT, OTHERS	Andy Paris
NARRATOR 3, PARKER, HARRIS, OTHERS	Troy Sostillio
NARRATOR 4, MAVOR, MARVIN TAYLOR, OTHERS	Greg Steinbruner

This production was subsequently transferred to the Minetta
Lane Theatre by Leonard Soloway and Chase Mishkin on
June 5, 1997, with the same cast.

CHARACTERS

OSCAR WILDE

LORD ALFRED DOUGLAS

SIR EDWARD CLARKE

EDWARD CARSON

MARQUESS OF QUEENSBERRY

The NARRATORS, who also play: PARKER, ATKINS, ALLEN, WOOD, MAVOR, QUEEN VICTORIA, POLICEMEN, GEORGE BERNARD SHAW, MR. GILL, MARVIN TAYLOR, MOISES KAUFMAN, NEWSPAPERMEN, JUDGES, etc.

The play can be performed with nine actors.

AUTHOR'S NOTE

This play has been inspired by techniques used by Erwin Piscator and the young Bertolt Brecht. In this regard, the performers should portray the characters in the play without "disappearing" into the parts.

Along the same lines, this play should be an actor-driven event. Costume changes, set changes, and anything else that happens on the stage should be done by actors.

The set is a performance space divided into two playing areas. One is an elevated stage that serves as a courtroom and other locations and the second is the area in front of that elevated stage. In this second area there is a long table covered with books from which the narrators quote. This area should be at the same level as the audience.

A note on the source material: When the text in the play comes from a historical account, the author and name of the book from which the text comes is stated by the narrators. There are two exceptions to this:

One is when there are several texts that come from different books by the same author. When this is the case, only the first book is mentioned.

Second, as the play progresses and Oscar Wilde's world collapses, so does this formal device. Therefore, in the second act not all sources are stated.

ACT I

PROLOGUE

The actors come onstage. The actor playing OSCAR WILDE *holds up a copy of* De Profundis *and reads:*

ACTOR: This is from *De Profundis* by Oscar Wilde:
"Do not be afraid of the past. If people tell you it is irrevocable, do not believe them. The past, present and future are but one moment in the sight of God. Time and space are merely accidental conditions of thought. The imagination can transcend them."

THE FIRST TRIAL

(The Judge's gavel)

NARRATOR 1: London, 3rd of April 1895. Old Bailey Central Criminal Court. Regina vs. Queensberry.

(Gavel)

NARRATOR 2 *(holding up the book):* The text of the trials are from the book *The Three Trials of Oscar Wilde*, compiled by H. Montgomery Hyde from shorthand notes from the trials. Other sources will be indicated. From *The Star:*

NARRATOR 4 *(holding up a newspaper):* Not for years has the Central Criminal Court at the Old Bailey been so densely crowded as it is today. People begged, bullied, and bribed for admission. . . .

(Gavel)

NARRATOR 1: Sir Edward Clarke, the opening speech for the prosecution:

(Gavel)

CLARKE: May it please you, my lord, gentlemen of the jury. We are here to try Lord Sholto Douglas, the 8th Marquess of Queensberry.

NARRATOR 1: Will the Marquess of Queensberry please stand.

CLARKE: The charge against him is that he published a false and malicious libel in regard to Mr. Oscar Wilde. The libel was published in the form of a card left by the Marquess at a club to which Mr. Oscar Wilde belonged. It is a visiting card of Lord Queensberry's with his name printed upon it.

NARRATOR 1: The court accepts it as Exhibit A.

CLARKE: The card has written upon it:

MARQUESS OF QUEENSBERRY: "Oscar Wilde: posing somdomite."

CLARKE: Of course it is a matter of serious moment that such a libel as that should in any way be connected with a gentleman who has borne a high reputation in this country.

NARRATOR 3: From *The Echo:*

NARRATOR 4: Several hours before the day's business opened at the Old Bailey this morning people were using every effort to gain admission to the old court. Never, perhaps, have so many prominent persons been disappointed to find their prominence would not serve them to gain entrance to a criminal court.

CLARKE: Mr. Wilde is a famous artist considered by many to be amongst the finest writers of this century. He represents a form of artistic literature which recommends itself to many of the foremost minds and the most cultivated people.

Mr. Wilde is a poet, a novelist, an essayist and a playwright. His last four plays have been great successes in the West End, and two of them are currently being performed there.

NARRATOR 3: From *The Evening News:*

NARRATOR 1: The importance of being early was never better illustrated than at the Old Bailey this morning when long before 10 o'clock every seat where a pressman could sit had a couple of competitors for it. . . .

CLARKE: The Marquess of Queensberry's claim to fame is that he patronized the man who designed the rules of boxing that bear his name: "The Queensberry Rules."

(Laughter in the court)

CARSON: My lord, I object.

JUDGE: Sir Edward, please.

CLARKE: Now, the words of the libel are not directly an accusation of the gravest of all offenses—the suggestion is that there was no guilt of the actual offense, but that in some way or other the person of whom those words were written did appear—nay, desired to appear—and pose to be a person guilty of or inclined to the commission of the gravest of all offenses.

You will appreciate that the leaving of such a card openly with the porter of a club is a most serious matter and one likely gravely to affect the position of the person as to whom that injurious suggestion was made.

NARRATOR 3: From *Reynolds* newspaper:

NARRATOR 2: The words written upon the card were of such character as to be unfit for publication.

CLARKE: But the matter does not stop at the question whether the card was delivered, or whether the defendant can in any way be excused by strong feeling—mistaken feeling—for having made that statement.

By the plea which the defendant has brought before the court, a much graver issue has been raised. In his plea of justification, the defendant has said that the statement is true and that it is for the public benefit that the statement was made.

It is for those who have put into the plea these serious allegations to prove to you, gentlemen of the jury, if they can, by credible witnesses, that these allegations are true.

Witnesses will be called who will prove the publication of the libel, and my learned friend has the task of satisfying you that there was enough justification for the publishing of that card.

NARRATOR 1: John Sholto Douglas, Marquess of Queensberry, how do you plead?

QUEENSBERRY: I plead not guilty, and also that the libel is true and that it is for the public benefit that it should be published. I wrote that card with the intention of bringing matters to a head, having been unable to meet Mr. Wilde otherwise, and to save my son, and I abide by what I wrote.

(Upheaval in the court. Three strikes of the gavel.)

NARRATOR 4: From *The Star:*

NARRATOR 3: This is without a doubt the trial of the century.

* * * * * *

NARRATOR 1: Mr. Oscar Wilde examined by Sir Edward Clarke:

(Gavel)

WILDE: I am the prosecutor in this case. I am thirty-nine years of age. My father was Sir William Wilde, surgeon of Dublin, and chairman of the Census Commission. I was a student at Trinity College, where I took a classical scholarship and the gold medal for Greek. I then went to Magdalen College, Oxford, where I took a classical scholarship, a first in "Mods" and a first in "Greats." There I also won the Newdigate Prize for English verse. I took my degree in 1878, and came down at once. From that time I have devoted myself to art and literature. In 1881, I published a volume of poems, and afterwards lectured in England and America. In 1884, I married Miss Constance Lloyd, and from that date until now have lived with her in Tite Street, Chelsea. I have two sons, the elder of whom will be ten in June and the second nine in November.

CLARKE: Mr. Wilde, you have published poetry, short stories, fairy tales for children, and the novel *The Picture of Dorian Gray*.

WILDE: Yes.

CLARKE: You have also toured America and Ireland lecturing on art, or more specifically, what you call the English Renaissance of Art.

NARRATOR 2: From a lecture to art students given in New York:

WILDE: I call it the English Renaissance of Art because it is indeed a sort of new birth of the spirit of man. Like the great Italian Renaissance of the fifteenth century, it possesses a desire for a more comely way of life, a passion for physical beauty, an exclusive attention to form. It seeks new subjects for poetry, new forms of art, new intellectual and imaginative enjoyments. In art as in politics there is but one origin to all revolutions, a desire on the part of man for a nobler form of life, for a freer method and opportunity of expression. This renaissance will create a new brotherhood among men by furnishing a universal language.

CLARKE: Mr. Wilde, you have also written several plays, two of which are currently being performed in the West End?

WILDE: Yes, *The Importance of Being Earnest* and *An Ideal Husband*.

CLARKE: When did you make the acquaintance of Lord Alfred Douglas?

WILDE: In 1891. He was brought to my house by a friend.

DOUGLAS: My first meeting with Oscar Wilde was an astonishment.

NARRATOR 3: From *The Autobiography of Lord Alfred Douglas*, written thirty years later:

DOUGLAS: I had never heard a man talking with such perfect sentences before, as if he had written them all overnight with labor and yet all spontaneous. He did succeed in weaving spells. It all appeared to be Wisdom and Power and Beauty and Enchantment. One sat and listened to him enthralled.

NARRATOR 4: From a letter written in January 1893:

WILDE: My own dear boy,
Your sonnet is quite lovely, and it is a marvel that those red rose lips of yours should be no less for music of song than for madness of kisses.

DOUGLAS: From the moment we met he made up to me in every possible way. He was continually asking me to dine or lunch with him. He flattered me, gave me presents and made much of me in every way. He gave me copies of all his books, with inscriptions in them.

WILDE: Your slim gilt soul walks between passion and poetry. I know Hyacinthus, whom Apollo loved so madly, was you in Greek days.

DOUGLAS: I was from the first flattered that a man as distinguished as he was should pay me so much attention and attach so much importance to all my views and preferences and whims.

WILDE: Why are you alone in London, and when do you go to Salisbury? Do go there to cool your hands in the gray twilight of gothic things, then come here whenever you like. It is a lovely place—it only lacks you.
Always with undying love,
Yours, Oscar.

DOUGLAS: I will say of him that even if he had never written a line of poetry, he would still be the most wonderful man I ever met.

CLARKE: When did Lord Alfred's father, the Marquess of Queensberry, first object to your relationship with his son?

WILDE: In April 1894, I saw a letter that he wrote to his son.

CLARKE: This is the letter in question. It was written on Sunday, 1st of April 1894, at the Carter's Hotel. It reads:

QUEENSBERRY: Alfred,
Your intimacy with this man Wilde. It must either cease or I'll disown you. I'm not going to try and analyze your intimacy, and I make no charge; but to my mind to pose as a thing is as bad as to be it. With my own eyes I saw you both in the most loathsome and disgusting relationship. Never in my experience have I seen such a sight as that in your horrible features. No wonder people are talking as they are. If I thought the actual thing was true, and it became public property, I should be quite justified in shooting him at sight. Your disgusted so-called father.

DOUGLAS: To Queensberry, Carter's Hotel, Albemarle Street:

NARRATOR 2: From a telegram written on the 2nd of April:

DOUGLAS: What a funny little man you are.

QUEENSBERRY: If you send me any more such telegrams, or come with any impertinence, I will give you the thrashing you deserve. If I catch you again with that man I'll make a public scandal that you little dream of. Unless this acquaintance ceases I shall carry out my threat and stop all supplies of money. So now you know what to expect.

CLARKE: What did you do when you learned that the Marquess of Queensberry objected to your friendship with his son?

WILDE: I said I was perfectly ready to cease the acquaintance if it would make peace between him and his father; but he preferred to do otherwise.

DOUGLAS: I treat your absurd threats with absolute indifference.

NARRATOR 2: From a letter written the next day:

DOUGLAS: I have made a point of appearing with Oscar Wilde at many public restaurants. I shall continue to go to any of these places whenever I choose and with whom I choose. If Oscar Wilde was to prosecute you in the Criminal Courts for your outrageous libel you would get seven years' penal servitude.

QUEENSBERRY: If I thought the actual thing was true, and it became public property, I should be quite justified in shooting him at sight. Right now I can only accuse him of posing.

DOUGLAS: If you try to assault me I shall defend myself with a loaded revolver which I always carry; and if I shoot you, or if he shoots you, we should be completely justified, as we should be acting in self-defense against a violent and dangerous rough. I think if you were dead not many people would miss you.

QUEENSBERRY: I received your telegram this morning by post from Carter's and have requested them not to forward any more, but just to tear any up, as I did yours, without reading it. You must be flush of money to waste it on such rubbish.

CLARKE: What happened next?

WILDE: At the end of June 1894, there was an interview between Lord Queensberry and myself in my house. He called upon me, not by appointment, at about four o'clock in the afternoon, accompanied by a gentleman with whom I was not acquainted. (As WILDE *narrates*, QUEENSBERRY *enters*.) The interview took place in my library. He said:

QUEENSBERRY: Sit down.

WILDE: I said: I do not allow anyone to talk like that to me in my house or anywhere else. I suppose you have come to apologize to me for the statements you made about me in that letter you wrote to your son. I should have the right any day I chose to prosecute you for writing such a letter.

QUEENSBERRY: The letter was privileged, as it was written to my son.

WILDE: How dare you say such things to him about us?

QUEENSBERRY: You were both kicked out of the Savoy Hotel at a moment's notice for your disgusting conduct.

WILDE: That is a lie.

QUEENSBERRY: You have taken furnished rooms for him in Piccadilly.

WILDE: Someone has been telling you an absurd set of lies. I have not done anything of the kind.

QUEENSBERRY: I hear you were thoroughly well blackmailed for a disgusting letter you wrote my son.

WILDE: That letter was a beautiful letter, and I never write except for publication. I said: Lord Queensberry, do you seriously accuse us of improper conduct? He replied:

QUEENSBERRY: I do not say that you are it, but you look it.

(Laughter in the court)

JUDGE: I shall have the court cleared if I hear the slightest disturbance again.

QUEENSBERRY: You look it, and you pose as it, which is just as bad. If I catch you and my son together again in any public restaurant I will thrash you.

WILDE: I do not know what the Queensberry rules are, but the Oscar Wilde rule is to shoot at sight. Leave my house.

QUEENSBERRY: I will not.

WILDE: I will have you put out by the police.

QUEENSBERRY: It is a disgusting scandal.

WILDE: If it be so, then you are the author of the scandal, and nobody else.
    I then went into the hall and pointed him out to my servant. This is the Marquess of Queensberry, the most infamous brute in London. You are never to allow him to enter my house again.

CARSON: So far as Lord Queensberry is concerned, any act he has done, in any letter he has written, he withdraws nothing.

NARRATOR 1: Edward Carson, the attorney for the defense:

CARSON: He has done all those things with a premeditation and a determination at all risks and at all hazards to save his son.

DOUGLAS: His so-called desire to save me is pure hypocrisy:

NARRATOR 2: From *The Autobiography of Lord Alfred Douglas*:

DOUGLAS: The real object is to persecute my mother and destroy me. My father is an inhuman brute, an atheist, and a lecher.

NARRATOR 4: From a letter Queensberry wrote to his son:

QUEENSBERRY: If you are my son, it is only confirming proof to me how right I was to face every horror and misery I have done rather than run the risk of bringing more creatures into the world like yourself. That was the entire and only reason for my breaking with your mother as a wife, so intensely dissatisfied was I with her as a mother to you children.

DOUGLAS: My mother divorced him; he harassed her for years and by turns neglected and ill treated us. He's despicable and mad.

QUEENSBERRY: No wonder you have fallen prey to this horrible brute. I am only sorry for you as a human creature.

NARRATOR 3: George Bernard Shaw on the Marquess of Queensberry:

SHAW: His pretended solicitude for his son and his alleged desire to save him were nothing but a hypocritical pretense. He was a Scots Marquess, Earl, Viscount, and Baron, with a fourfold contempt for public opinion, an ungovernable temper, and after his divorce, a maniacal hatred for his family. His real objective was to ruin his son and to finally break the heart of his ex-wife.

DOUGLAS: My entire family is with you Oscar. You must prosecute.

NARRATOR 3: From Clarke's unpublished memoirs of the trial:

CLARKE: Mr. Wilde, you've told me you are considerably in debt. Who will carry the cost of these proceedings?

DOUGLAS: My family will be delighted to pay for all the necessary costs. My father has been an incubus to us all. We have often discussed the possibility of getting him into a lunatic asylum. He is a daily source of annoyance to my mother and everyone else. My family will be only too delighted to pay for all costs and expenses to try my father.

NARRATOR: From *De Profundis:*

WILDE: Of course his family never paid for the costs of the trial.

QUEENSBERRY: You must all be mad, and if you make inquiries, you will find that the whole town has been reeking of this hideous scandal of Oscar Wilde for the past three years.

CLARKE: When was your next encounter with the Marquess of Queensberry?

WILDE: It was at the St. James Theatre on the opening night of the play *The Importance of Being Earnest.*
    Lord Queensberry had booked a seat for the performance.

NARRATOR 1: From a letter to Lord Alfred Douglas:

WILDE: Dearest Boy,
    Yes, the Scarlet Marquis made a plot to address the audience on the first night of my play! Henry Bourke re-

vealed it, and I had all Scotland Yard to guard the theater. When your father arrived there—with a prize fighter—the police did not allow him to enter.

CLARKE: The disturbance on the opening night of a new play could be a very serious matter to author and actors, and it would have been especially serious if it had developed into a personal attack on the private character of Mr. Wilde.

WILDE: He prowled about for three hours, then left chattering like some monstrous ape.
    He left a grotesque bouquet of vegetables for me! This of course makes his conduct idiotic, robs it of dignity.

CLARKE: The Marquess had done this in another theater on the night of the performance of a play. Not one by Mr. Wilde, but one that dealt with religious issues. At a certain moment in the play, as a character talked about religion, the Marquess got up from his seat and began shouting at the actor on stage. I encourage you to imagine the consequences of such behavior on the opening night of a new play.

CLARKE: What happened next?

WILDE: On the 28th of February I went to the Albemarle Club and received from the porter the card which has been produced.

NARRATOR 1: The court calls Sidney Wright.

WRIGHT: I am the hall porter at the Albemarle Club. Mr. and Mrs. Wilde are members of the club. On the 18th of

February the Marquess of Queensberry came to the club and said:

QUEENSBERRY: I'm here to see Oscar Wilde.

WRIGHT: When I informed him he was not there, the Marquess wrote a note on a card and said:

QUEENSBERRY: Give that to Mr. Wilde.

WRIGHT *(He reads the card.):* When Mr. Wilde came to the club on the 28th of February, I handed it to him. *(He does.)* He read it and appeared very distraught by its content.

QUEENSBERRY: Oscar Wilde, posing somdomite.

WILDE *(showing the card to* WRIGHT*):* The Marquess's spelling is somewhat unusual.

NARRATOR 1: From a letter to his friend Robert Ross, written that night:

WILDE: Dearest Robie:
    Something has happened. Bosie's father has left a card at my club with hideous words on it. I can see nothing but a criminal prosecution. My whole life seems ruined by this man. I don't know what to do.

NARRATOR 4: From *Oscar Wilde* by Frank Harris. An account of their meeting at the Café Royal:

HARRIS: Oscar, Bernard Shaw is lunching with me tomorrow at the Café Royal. Come at three o'clock and meet us there.

NARRATOR 2: George Bernard Shaw:

SHAW: Wilde came in and told us the story of the conflict.
He finished by saying that he was taking the Marquess of Queensberry to court.

WILDE: I'm bringing an action against Queensberry, Frank, for criminal libel. He is a mere wild beast.

HARRIS: Oscar, you must not do anything of the kind.

WILDE: My solicitors tell me that some of the things I have written will be brought up against me in court. Now, you know all I have written. Would you in your position as editor of *The Fortnightly* come and give evidence for me, testify that *Dorian Gray* is not an immoral book?

HARRIS: Yes. I am perfectly willing, and I can say more than that; I can say that you are one of the very few men I have ever known whose talk and whose writing were vowed away from grossness of any sort.

WILDE: Oh, Frank, would you?

SHAW: He was almost in tears.

WILDE: It would be most kind of you. Your evidence will win the case.

HARRIS: Anything I can do, Oscar, I shall do with pleasure. But I want you to consider the matter carefully. An English law court is all very well for two average men who are fighting an ordinary business dispute. That is what it is made for, but to judge the morality or immorality of an artist is to ask the court to do what it is wholly unfit to do.

WILDE: My solicitors tell me I shall win.

HARRIS: Solicitors live on quarrels. Let us begin by putting the law courts out of the question. Don't forget that if you lose and Queensberry goes free, everyone will hold that you have been guilty of nameless vice. The Crown could charge you with gross indecency and send you to two years hard labor. You must know that that could happen. You could go to prison for two years.

WILDE: But Frank . . .

HARRIS: You must remember that you are a standard-bearer for future generations. You are an artist and a revolutionary. If you lose you will make it harder for all writers in England. God knows it's hard enough already, but you will put back the hands of the clock by fifty years.

WILDE: What should I do?

HARRIS: You should go abroad, and as ace of trumps, you should take your wife with you.

WILDE: You are right of course, Frank. You know it's Bosie who wants me to fight his father.

HARRIS: Let Queensberry and his son fight out their own miserable quarrels; they are well matched.

WILDE: Oh, Frank, how can I do that?

SHAW: I think it was about this time that Bosie Douglas came in.

DOUGLAS: The day of the lunch at the Café Royal I was very anxious that the case against my father would proceed and I resented any arguments in favor of its abandonment. I was terribly afraid that Oscar would weaken and throw up the sponge.

SHAW: At Oscar's request Harris repeated his argument and to my astonishment Douglas got up at once and said:

DOUGLAS: Such advice shows you are no friend of Oscar's.

HARRIS: What do you mean?

SHAW: He turned and left the room on the spot. Then, Oscar got up and said:

WILDE: It is not friendly of you, Frank. It really is not friendly.

SHAW: And he too left the room.

HARRIS: I turned to Shaw and said: Did I say anything in the heat of the argument that would have offended Oscar or Douglas?

SHAW: Nothing, not a word; you have nothing to reproach yourself with.

DOUGLAS: I stormed out of the restaurant because I feared I might not be able to convince you and Mr. Shaw and that you would argue Wilde out of the state of mind I had gotten him into.

QUEENSBERRY: You reptile!

HARRIS: Once Douglas left I was suddenly struck by a sort of likeness, a similarity of expression and of temper between Lord Alfred Douglas and his unhappy father. I could not get it out of my head: that little face blanched with rage and the wild, hating eyes, the shrill voice, too, was Queensberry's.

QUEENSBERRY: You are no son of mine and I never thought you were.

HARRIS: One thing was clear from our meeting. Lord Alfred had set his mind on Wilde prosecuting his father. It seemed as if he knew exactly how that was to be done.

DOUGLAS: Sir Edward, you must put me in the witness box and allow me to testify against my father.

NARRATOR 1: From *The Autobiography of Lord Alfred Douglas:*

DOUGLAS: If not, we might as well throw up the case at once. He said:

CLARKE: Make your mind at rest, Lord Alfred, I agree with everything you say. My idea of the way to conduct this case is to launch out at the very outset with a deadly attack on

Lord Queensberry for his conduct to his family, of which we have ample proof in his letters to you.

DOUGLAS: I said: Yes, but you must promise faithfully you will put me in the box.
He replied:

CLARKE: I promise you I will; you shall go into the box immediately after my opening speech.

NARRATOR 2: From the unpublished memoirs of the trial by Sir Edward Clarke:

CLARKE: I made no such agreement or promise.

NARRATOR 2: A warrant for the arrest of Lord Sholto Douglas, the 8th Marquess of Queensberry, was issued the next day.

(Three strikes of the gavel)

CLARKE: In his plea of justification, submitted by the Marquess of Queensberry, he has said that the statement made in his card is true, and that it was made for the public benefit.

In support of this plea he puts forth, amongst other things, the following proof: first, that Mr. Wilde published or caused to have published a magazine entitled *The Chameleon*, relating to the practices of persons of unnatural habit.

And second, that Mr. Wilde published or caused to have published a certain immoral and indecent book with the title *The Picture of Dorian Gray*. The Marquess alleges that this book describes the relations, intimacies, and passions of certain persons guilty of unnatural practices.

Gentlemen of the jury, it would appear, according to this plea of justification, that what is on trial here is not the Marquess of Queensberry but Mr. Wilde's art.

Mr. Wilde, it is suggested that you are responsible for the publication of the magazine *The Chameleon*, on the front page of which some aphorisms of yours appear. Beyond sending that contribution, had you anything to do with the preparation or publication of the magazine?

WILDE: No. Nothing whatever.

CLARKE: The other question relates to the book *The Picture of Dorian Gray*. These are some of the reviews of *Dorian Gray: The Speaker:*

NARRATOR 2: A work of serious art.

CLARKE: *The Glasgow Herald:*

NARRATOR 1: The book is a delight to the hand and the eye.

CLARKE: *The Echo:*

NARRATOR 4: The end suffered by Dorian Gray, his disintegration into a heap of muck, is the only right punishment for a man of his nature. Mr. Wilde has written the most moral book of this century.

CLARKE: Mr. Wilde, would you care to add anything?

WILDE: No.

CLARKE: In the next part of the plea of justification submitted by the Marquess of Queensberry, he names several young men and impugns your character with them. You have read the plea?

WILDE: Yes.

CLARKE: Is there any truth in any of these accusations?

WILDE: There is no truth whatever in any one of them.

CLARKE: My lord, nothing more with this witness.

(Three strikes of the gavel)

NARRATOR 1: Oscar Wilde cross-examined by Edward Carson:

CARSON: Lord Queensberry's conduct has been absolutely consistent all through, and if the facts which he stated in his letters as to Mr. Wilde's reputation and acts are correct, then not only was he justified in doing what he could to cut short what would probably prove to be a most disastrous acquaintance for his son, but in taking every step which suggested itself to him to bring about an inquiry into the acts and doings of Mr. Wilde. You stated that your age was thirty-nine. I think you are over forty.

WILDE: I have no wish to pose as being young. I am thirty-nine or forty. You have my certificate and that should settle the matter.

CARSON: You were born on the 16th of October 1854. That makes you more than forty.

WILDE: Ah! Very well.

CARSON: What age is Lord Alfred Douglas?

WILDE: Lord Alfred Douglas is about twenty-four, and was between twenty and twenty-one years of age when I first knew him.

CARSON: I hold in my hand a letter written by Mr. Wilde to Lord Alfred Douglas; I will now read it for the court.

My own dear Boy,
    Your sonnet is quite lovely, and it is a marvel that those red rose lips of yours should have been made no less for music of song than for madness of kisses. Your slim gilt soul walks between passion and poetry. I know Hyacinthus, whom Apollo loved so madly, was you in Greek days.
    Why are you alone in London, and when do you go to Salisbury? Do go there to cool your hands in the gray twilight of gothic things, then came here whenever you like. It is a lovely place—it only lacks you.
    Always with undying love,
    Yours,
    Oscar

Why should a man of your age address a boy nearly twenty years younger as "My own boy"?

WILDE: I was fond of him. I have always been fond of him.
    Sir, this is a beautiful letter. It is a poem. I was not writ-

ing an ordinary letter. You might as well cross-examine me as to whether *King Lear* or a sonnet of Shakespeare's is proper.

CARSON: Apart from art, Mr. Wilde?

WILDE: I cannot answer apart from art.

CARSON: Suppose a man who was not an artist had written this letter, would you say it was a proper letter?

WILDE: A man who was not an artist could not have written that letter.

CARSON: Why?

WILDE: Because nobody but an artist could write it. He certainly could not write the language unless he were a man of letters.

CARSON: I can suggest, for the sake of your reputation, that there is nothing very wonderful in this "red rose lips of yours"?

WILDE: A great deal depends on the way it is read.

CARSON: "Your slim gilt soul walks between passion and poetry." Is that a beautiful phrase?

WILDE: Not as you read it, Mr. Carson. You read it very badly.

CARSON: I do not profess to be an artist; and when I hear you give evidence, I am glad I am not.

CLARKE: I object, my lord. I don't think my friend should talk like that.

JUDGE: Sustained. Mr. Carson, please.

CLARKE *(to* WILDE*):* Pray, do not criticize my friend's reading again.

CARSON: Here is another letter which I believe you also wrote to Lord Alfred Douglas. Will you read it?

WILDE: No, I decline. I don't see why I should.

CARSON: Then I will.

NARRATOR 1: From a letter written at the Savoy Hotel:

CARSON: Dearest of all boys,
    Your letter was delightful, red and yellow wine to me; but I am sad and out of sorts. Bosie, you must not make scenes with me. They kill me, they wreck the loveliness of life. I cannot see you, so Greek and gracious, distorted with passion. I cannot listen to your curved lips saying hideous things to me. I would sooner die than have you bitter, unjust, hating. . . . I must see you soon. You are the divine thing I want, the thing of grace and beauty, but I don't know how to do it. I have also got a new sitting-room. . . . Why are you not here, my dear, my wonderful boy?
    Your own Oscar.

Is that an ordinary letter?

WILDE: Everything I write is extraordinary. I do not pose as being ordinary, great heavens! Ask me any question you like about it.

CARSON: Is it the kind of letter that a man writes to another?

WILDE: It was a tender expression of my great admiration for Lord Alfred Douglas.

CARSON *(holding a magazine in his hand):* Mr. Wilde, this is the magazine *The Chameleon?*

WILDE: Yes.

CARSON: Why did you contribute your writings to *The Chameleon?*

WILDE: I was asked by a friend to do so.

CARSON: Would that friend be Lord Alfred Douglas?

WILDE: Yes.

CARSON: Why would he want you to contribute to this magazine?

WILDE: The publishers of the magazine are friends of his at Oxford. *The Chameleon* is an Oxford undergraduate publication.

CARSON: Lord Alfred Douglas himself also contributed to this issue of the magazine. Two poems, I believe.

WILDE: Yes. Two very beautiful poems.

CARSON: In the magazine, in addition to your contribution and the two poems by Lord Alfred Douglas, there is a short story entitled *(reading)* "The Priest and the Acolyte." In it a priest falls in love with a boy who serves him at the altar, and is discovered by the rector in the priest's room. Then scandal arises. Have you read "The Priest and the Acolyte"?

WILDE: Yes.

CARSON: You have no doubt whatever that that was an improper story?

WILDE: From a literary point of view it was highly improper. It would be impossible for a man of literature to judge it otherwise; by literature I mean treatment, selection of subject, and the like. I thought the treatment rotten and the subject rotten.

CARSON: You are of the opinion, I believe, that there is no such thing as an immoral book?

WILDE: That is correct.

CARSON: May I take it you think "The Priest and the Acolyte" was not immoral?

WILDE: It was worse. It was badly written.

CARSON: Did you think the story blasphemous?

WILDE: The story filled me with disgust. The end was wrong.

CARSON: Answer the question, sir. Did you or did you not consider the story blasphemous?

WILDE: I thought it horrible. "Blasphemous" is not a word of mine.

In writing a play or a book, I am concerned entirely with literature, that is, with art. I aim not at doing good or evil, but at making a thing that will have some quality of beauty.

CARSON: This is your contribution to *The Chameleon*. "Phrases and Philosophies for the Use of the Young."

This is one of those phrases: "Wickedness is a myth invented by good people to account for the curious attractiveness of others." You think that true?

WILDE: I rarely think that anything I write is true.

CARSON: Did you say "rarely"?

WILDE: I said "rarely." I might have said "never"—not true in the actual sense of the word.

CARSON: "If one tells the truth, one is sure, sooner or later, to be found out."

WILDE: That is a pleasing paradox, but I do not set very high store on it as an axiom.

CARSON: Is it good for the young?

WILDE: Anything is good that stimulates thought in any age.

CARSON: Whether moral or immoral?

WILDE: There is no such thing as morality or immorality in thought.

CARSON: "Pleasure is the only thing one should live for."

WILDE: I think that the realization of oneself is the prime aim in life, and to realize oneself through pleasure is surely finer than to do so through pain. I am, on that point, entirely on the side of the ancients—the Greeks. It is a pagan idea.

CARSON: "A truth ceases to be true when more than one person believes in it."

WILDE: Perfectly. That would be my metaphysical definition of truth: something so personal that the same truth could never be appreciated by two minds.

CARSON: What would you say would be the effect of "Phrases and Philosophies" taken in connection with such an article as "The Priest and the Acolyte"?

WILDE: Undoubtedly, it was the idea that might be formed that made me object so strongly to the story. I saw at once that maxims that were perfectly nonsensical, paradoxical, or whatever you like, might be read in conjunction with it.

CARSON: I will now move to *The Picture of Dorian Gray.* These are some other reviews of *Dorian Gray. The Scottish Leader:*

NARRATOR 3: The novel portrays the gilded paganism which has been staining these later years of Victorian epoch with horrors that carry us back to the worst incidents in the history of ancient Rome.

CARSON: *The St. James Gazette:*

NARRATOR 4: *The Picture of Dorian Gray* is a stupid and vulgar piece of work. Not wishing to offend the nostrils of decent persons, we do not propose to analyze it. Suffice it to say that it is dangerous and corrupt.

NARRATOR 1: From *The Soul of Man Under Socialism:*

WILDE: In the old days, men had the rack. Now they have the press.

CARSON: This is from your introduction to *Dorian Gray:* "There is no such thing as a moral or an immoral book. Books are well written or badly written." That expresses your view?

WILDE: My view on art, yes.

CARSON: Then may I take it that no matter how immoral a book may be, if it is well written, it is, in your opinion, a good book?

WILDE: Yes, if it were well written so as to produce a sense of beauty, which is the highest sense of which a human being can be capable. If it were badly written, it would produce a sense of disgust.

CARSON: A perverted novel might be a good book?

WILDE: I don't know what you mean by a "perverted" novel.

CARSON: Then I will suggest *Dorian Gray* as open to the interpretation of being such a novel?

WILDE: That could only be to brutes and illiterates. The views of Philistines are entirely unaccountable.

CARSON: *The St. James Gazette:*

NARRATOR 4: Mr. Wilde says that his story is a moral tale, because the wicked persons in it come to a bad end.

WILDE: I never said my characters were wicked.

NARRATOR 4: In this newspaper's opinion, the work is unredeemed because it constantly hints, not obscurely, at disgusting sins and abominable crimes.

WILDE: The books that the world calls immoral are the books that show the world its own shame.

CARSON: I will now proceed to read from *Dorian Gray*. This is from the segment when the painter Basil Hallward meets Dorian Gray *(reading):*

> . . . The story is simply this. Two months ago I went to a crush at Lady Brandon's. Well, after I had been in the room about ten minutes, talking to huge overdressed dowagers and tedious Academicians, I suddenly became conscious that someone was looking at me.

(These last four words are spoken by both WILDE *and* CARSON *as* WILDE *takes over narrating the story.)*

WILDE: I turned half-way round and saw Dorian Gray for the first time. When our eyes met, I felt that I was growing pale. A curious instinct of terror came over me. I knew that I had come face to face with someone whose mere personality was so fascinating that, if I allowed it to do so, it would absorb my whole nature, my whole soul, my very art itself. I grew afraid, and turned to quit the room. It was not courage that made me do so: it was cowardice. I take no credit to myself for trying to escape.

I struggled towards the door. There, of course, I stumbled against Lady Brandon. "You are not going to turn away so soon, Mr. Hallward?" she screamed out. You know her shrill horrid voice? She is a peacock in everything but beauty.

I could not get rid of her. She brought me up to the royalties, and people with Stars and Garters, and elderly ladies with gigantic tiaras and parrot noses.

Suddenly I found myself face to face with the young man whose personality had so strangely stirred me.

CARSON *(taking over the narration):* We were quite close, almost touching. Our eyes met again. It was reckless of me, but I asked Lady Brandon to introduce me to him.
    The Pall Mall Gazette:

NARRATOR 3: *The Picture of Dorian Gray* ought to be chucked into the fire.

WILDE: To say that such a book as mine ought to be chucked into the fire is silly. That's what one does with newspapers.

CARSON: Here's another section:

I see Dorian every day now. I couldn't be happy if I didn't see him every day. Of course, sometimes it is only for a few minutes, but a few minutes with somebody one worships is worth a great deal.

WILDE *(taking over the narration):* It is quite true that I have worshipped you with far more romance of feeling than a man usually gives to a friend. From the moment we met, your personality had the most extraordinary influence over me. I quite admit that I adored you madly, extravagantly, absurdly. I was jealous of everyone to whom you spoke. I wanted to have you all to myself. I was only happy when I was with you. When I was away from you, you were still present in my art.

One day I determined to paint a wonderful portrait of you. It was to have been my masterpiece. It is my masterpiece. But, as I worked it, each flake and film of color seemed to me to reveal my secret.

CARSON *(taking over the narration):* I grew afraid that the world would know of my idolatry. I felt, Dorian, that I had told too much. Then, it was that I resolved never to allow the picture to be exhibited. The picture must not be shown.

Do you mean to say that that passage describes the natural feeling of one man towards another?

WILDE: It would be the influence produced by a beautiful personality.

CARSON: A beautiful person?

WILDE: I said "a beautiful personality." You can describe it as you like. Dorian Gray's was a most remarkable personality.

CARSON: May I take it that you, as an artist, have never known the feeling you described here?

WILDE: I have never allowed any personality to dominate my art.

CARSON: Then you have never known the feeling you described?

WILDE: No. It is a work of fiction.

CARSON: But let us go over it phrase by phrase. "I quite admit that I adored you madly." What do you have to say to that? Have you ever adored a young man madly?

WILDE: No, not madly. I prefer love—that is a higher form.

CARSON: Never mind about that. Let us keep down to the level we are at now.

WILDE: I have never given adoration to anybody except myself.

CARSON: Then you have never had that feeling?

WILDE: No. The whole idea was borrowed from Shakespeare, I regret to say—yes, from Shakespeare's sonnets.

CARSON: "I grew jealous of everyone to whom you spoke." Have you ever been jealous of a young man?

WILDE: Never in my life.

CARSON: "I wanted to have you all to myself." Have you ever had that feeling?

WILDE: No. I should consider it a nuisance, an intense bore.

CARSON: "I grew afraid that the world would know of my idolatry." Why should he grow afraid that the world should know of it?

WILDE: Because there are people in the world who cannot understand the intense devotion, affection, and admiration that an artist can feel for a wonderful and beautiful personality. These are the conditions under which we live. I regret them.

CARSON: These unfortunate people, who have not the high understanding that you have, might put it down to something wrong?

WILDE: Undoubtedly.

(Three strikes of the gavel)

NARRATOR 3: Thursday, 4th of April 1895. The second day of the trial.
From *The Evening News:*

NARRATOR 1: Today is the second day of the hearing of the prosecution of the Marquess of Queensberry for criminal libel by Oscar Wilde.
The fame of yesterday's performance, for it was little else, has gone abroad. Newspapers around the world have front page stories on the trial. In Paris, *Le Temps:*

NARRATOR 4: This is how the English behave with their poets.

NARRATOR 1: *The New York Herald:*

NARRATOR 2: This is how English poets behave.

NARRATOR 1: Today the cross-examination intends to leave the literary plane and penetrate the dim-lit, perfumed rooms where the poet of the beautiful joined with valets and grooms in the bond of silver cigarette cases.

DOUGLAS: My father used the period right before the trial to hire two detectives to round up men who had been with Oscar.

NARRATOR 3: From *The Autobiography of Lord Alfred Douglas:*

DOUGLAS: These men were warned that unless they testified against Oscar, they themselves would be taken to court.

NARRATOR 2: The court is in session.

(Three strikes of the gavel)

CARSON: Lord Queensberry learned that Wilde had been going about with young men who were not co-equal with him in social position or in age. These men, it will be proved beyond doubt, are some of the most immoral characters in London.

I refer above all to the man Alfred Taylor, a most notorious character—as the police will tell the court—who occupied rooms which were nothing more or less than a shameful den. Mr. Wilde, do you know Alfred Taylor?

WILDE: Yes.

CARSON: Is he an intimate friend of yours?

WILDE: I do not call him an intimate friend. He was a friend of mine. I have been several times to his house, some seven or eight times, perhaps.

CARSON: You used to go to tea parties there, afternoon tea parties?

WILDE: Yes.

CARSON: Did his rooms strike you as being peculiar?

WILDE: No, except that he displayed more than usual taste.

CARSON: Not the sort of street you would usually visit. You had no other friends there?

WILDE: No, this was merely a bachelor's place.

CARSON: Rather a rough neighborhood.

WILDE: That I don't know. I know it was near the Houses of Parliament.

CARSON: Taylor burned incense, did he not?

WILDE: Pastilles, I think.

CARSON: Incense, I suggest.

WILDE: I think not, pastilles, I should say. In those little Japanese things that run along rods.

CARSON: Did you know that Taylor had a lady's costume—a lady's fancy dress—in his rooms?

WILDE: No.

CARSON: Did you ever see him with one on?

WILDE: No. I was never told he had such dresses. He is a man of great taste and intelligence, and I know he was brought up at a good English school.

CARSON: Now, did you know that Taylor was being watched by the police?

WILDE: No, I never heard that.

CARSON: Did you know that Taylor was notorious for introducing young men to older men?

WILDE: I never heard that in my life.

CARSON: Did you get him to arrange dinners at which you could meet young men?

WILDE: No.

CARSON: But you have dined with young men?

WILDE: Often.

CARSON: Did you meet Charles Parker at his house?

WILDE: Yes. I met him at tea there.

CARSON: Did you ever meet a man named Sidney Mavor there?

WILDE: Yes.

CARSON: Did you meet Fred Atkins there?

WILDE: Yes.

CARSON: How many men has Alfred Taylor introduced you to?

WILDE: About five.

CARSON: Were these young men all about twenty?

WILDE: Yes; twenty or twenty-two.

CARSON: What was their occupation?

WILDE: I do not know if these particular young men had occupations.

CARSON: Have you given money to them?

WILDE: Yes. I think to all five—money or presents.

CARSON: What was there in common between these young men and yourself? What attraction had they for you?

WILDE: I delight in the society of people much younger than myself. I like those who may be called idle or careless. I recognize no social distinctions at all of any kind; and to me youth, the mere fact of youth, is so wonderful that I would sooner talk to a young man for half-an-hour than be—well, cross-examined in court.

NARRATOR 2: From *Lord Alfred Douglas* by H. Montgomery Hyde:

In the first interview between Sir Edward Clarke and Oscar Wilde, Clarke said:

CLARKE: Mr. Wilde, I can only accept this brief, if you assure me on your honor that there is not and never has been any foundation for the charges that are made against you.

WILDE: They are absolutely groundless.

CLARKE: So you give me your word as an English gentleman.

WILDE: I do.

NARRATOR 2: The thing that Clarke overlooked is that Wilde was an Irishman.

NARRATOR 3: This promise was made in the presence of Lord Alfred Douglas, who never thought to deny it or to alert Oscar to the danger he faced if the lie was disproved in court.

NARRATOR 4: Lord Alfred Douglas was asked years later if Wilde often denied his homosexuality.

DOUGLAS: Oscar was never in the least degree ashamed of his homosexuality. Of course we didn't have that word back then. But he talked openly about his desire for men. He gloried in it. He never denied it except, as George Bernard Shaw points out, "when legal fictions were necessary in the courts of law."

CARSON: Among these five did Taylor introduce you to Charles Parker?

WILDE: Yes, he was one with whom I became friendly.

CARSON: How old was Mr. Parker?

WILDE: He was twenty years old.

CARSON: Where did you first meet him?

WILDE: At Kettner's. It was Taylor's birthday, and I asked him to dinner, telling him to bring any of his friends. He brought the two Parkers.

CARSON: Did you know that Charles Parker was a gentleman's valet, and the other a groom?

WILDE: I did not know it, but if I had I should not have cared. I didn't care two pence what they were. I liked them.

CARSON: Taylor accepted your invitation by inviting a valet and a groom to dine with you?

WILDE: That would be your account, not mine.

CARSON: What did you have for dinner?

WILDE: Well, I really can't recall the menu.

CARSON: Was it a good dinner?

WILDE: Yes, certainly.

CARSON: All for the valet and the groom?

WILDE: No, for my friends and for Mr. Taylor, whose birthday it was.

CARSON: You did the honors to the valet and the groom?

WILDE: I entertained Mr. Taylor and his two guests.

CARSON: In a private room, of course.

WILDE: Yes, certainly.

CARSON: You had wine?

WILDE: Of course.

CARSON: Was there plenty of champagne?

WILDE: Well, I did not press wine upon them.

CARSON: You did not stint them?

WILDE: What gentleman would stint his guests?

CARSON: What gentleman would stint the valet and the groom?

CLARKE: I object, my lord . . .

CARSON: I withdraw the question. Do you drink champagne yourself?

WILDE: Yes, iced champagne is a favorite drink of mine—strongly against my doctor's orders.

CARSON: Never mind your doctor's orders, sir.

WILDE: I never do.

CARSON: After dinner, did you drive Charles Parker to the Savoy Hotel?

WILDE: No, he never went with me to the Savoy at all.

CARSON: Did any improprieties take place between you and Mr. Parker?

WILDE: No, none whatsoever.

CARSON: When did you first meet Fred Atkins?

WILDE: In October 1892.

CARSON: How old was he?

WILDE: He was about nineteen or twenty.

CARSON: You dined with him?

WILDE: Yes.

CARSON: Did you give Atkins a cigarette case?

WILDE: Yes. I found him a pleasant, good-humored companion.

CARSON: Did you give Atkins any money?

WILDE: Yes, £3 15s. to buy his first song for the music-hall stage.

CARSON: Did improprieties ever take place between you and Atkins?

WILDE: No, none whatsoever.

CARSON: You knew a man named Ernest Scarfe?

WILDE: Yes.

CARSON: How old is he?

WILDE: He is a young man of about twenty.

CARSON: You had dinner with him?

WILDE: Yes.

CARSON: Did you give Scarfe any money?

WILDE: Never.

CARSON: Did you give him any presents?

WILDE: Yes, a cigarette case.

CARSON: When did you first know Sidney Mavor?

WILDE: In September 1892.

CARSON: Did you give Mavor any money?

WILDE: No. I gave him a cigarette case.

CARSON: Do you know Walter Grainger?

WILDE: Yes.

CARSON: How old is he?

WILDE: He was about sixteen when I knew him.

CARSON: What was his occupation?

WILDE: He was a servant at a certain house in Height Street.

CARSON: Did you ever kiss him?

WILDE: Oh, dear no. He was a peculiarly plain boy. He was, unfortunately, extremely ugly. I pitied him for it.

(The court falls silent. Pause.)

CARSON: Was that the reason why you did not kiss him?

WILDE: Oh, Mr. Carson, you are impertinently insolent.

CARSON: Did you say that in support of your statement that you never kissed him?

WILDE: No. It is a childish question.

CARSON: Did you ever put that forward as a reason why you never kissed the boy?

WILDE: No, not at all.

CARSON: Why, sir, did you mention that this boy was extremely ugly?

WILDE: For this reason. If I were asked why I did not kiss a doormat, I should say because I do not like to kiss doormats. I do not know why I mentioned that he was ugly, except that I was stung by the insolent question you had put to me and the way you have insulted me throughout this hearing.

CARSON: Why did you mention his ugliness?

WILDE: It is ridiculous to imagine that any such thing could have occurred under any circumstances.

CARSON: Then why did you mention his ugliness, I ask you?

WILDE: Perhaps I was insulted by an insulting question.

CARSON: Is that a reason why you should say the boy was ugly?

WILDE: No, I said it because . . . (WILDE *can't find the words to continue.*)

CARSON: Why?

WILDE: Because I didn't . . . (WILDE *can't find the words to continue.*)

CARSON: Why?

WILDE: Because . . .

CARSON: Why did you say that?

WILDE: You sting me and insult me and try to unnerve me; and at times one says things flippantly when one ought to speak more seriously. I admit that.

CARSON: Then you said it flippantly?

WILDE: Oh, yes, it was a flippant answer.

CARSON: I'm done with this witness, my lord.

WILDE: No indecencies ever took place between myself and Grainger. I went down . . .

CARSON: I'm finished with this witness, my lord!

CLARKE: My lord, this is the case for the prosecution.

DOUGLAS: I can't believe this!

NARRATOR 1: From *Oscar Wilde: A Summing Up* by Lord Alfred Douglas:

DOUGLAS: If Sir Edward Clarke had not gone back on his solemn promise to put me in the witness box so that I could testify against my father . . .

CLARKE: Lord Douglas's testimony would not have helped.

NARRATOR 2: From Clarke's unpublished memoirs of the trials:

CLARKE: Lord Queensberry's character was not on trial here, and it was quite irrelevant to the case. The legal argument was concerned purely and simply with whether or not the Marquess could justify his libel in a court of law.

NARRATOR 4: From *Oscar Wilde* by Sheridan Morley:

CLARKE: Wilde and I decided that Alfred Douglas should not be called as a witness. It would look quite bad to have Queensberry attacked by his own child.

DOUGLAS: If I had got into the witness box I probably would have saved Oscar, because in the first place, I was a first-class witness, and in the second place, it would have been impossible for Carson to cross-examine me in a hostile way without exposing the hypocrisy of my father and establishing the truth.

NARRATOR 4: For the rest of his life Lord Alfred Douglas would regret not having been called to the witness box.

CLARKE: The case for the prosecution is closed, my lord. I reserve to myself the power to call evidence to rebut anything that may be sprung on me.

(Three strikes of the gavel)

NARRATOR 1: Edward Carson, The opening speech for the defense:

(Three strikes of the gavel)

CARSON: Gentlemen, from beginning to end Lord Queensberry, in dealing with Mr. Oscar Wilde, has been influenced by one hope alone: that of saving his son.

In my judgment, even if the case had rested on Mr. Wilde's art and literature alone, Lord Queensberry would have been absolutely justified in the course he has taken. Lord Queensberry has undertaken to prove that Mr. Wilde has been "posing" as guilty of certain vices.

I am not here to say anything has ever happened between Lord Alfred Douglas and Mr. Oscar Wilde. God forbid! But everything shows that the young man was in a dangerous position in that he acquiesced to the domination of Mr. Wilde, a man of great ability and attainments.

DOUGLAS: That's absurd.

NARRATOR 3: From *Oscar Wilde, A Summing Up*, written forty years later:

DOUGLAS: After I had known Oscar for about nine months, I did with him and allowed him to do with me just what was done among boys at Winchester and Oxford. He treated me as an older boy treats a younger one at school. He also taught me things that were new to me.

CARSON: Against this Lord Queensberry protested; and I wish to know, gentlemen, are you, for that protest, going to send Lord Queensberry to jail?

I will now proceed with the most painful part of the case. I will introduce you to a series of young men who will testify under oath that Mr. Oscar Wilde solicited their services in committing acts of the grossest indecency.

You will hear from Charles Parker. He will tell you that Mr. Wilde committed acts of gross indecency with him. You will hear from Alfred Wood. He too will tell you that Mr. Wilde paid him to commit these acts with him.

You will hear from William Parker, you will hear from Sidney Mavor, you will hear from Fred Atkins. You will hear these men testify that Mr. Wilde committed acts of the grossest indecency with them. You will hear from their lips . . .

(CARSON *continues with his text*, sotto voce.)

NARRATOR 2: At this point Clarke was seen to leave the court with Wilde.

From *Lord Alfred Douglas* by H. Montgomery Hyde:

CLARKE: Mr. Wilde, it is almost impossible in view of all the circumstances to induce a jury to convict of a criminal offense a father who was endeavoring to save his son from an evil companionship. I see no hope at all of a guilty verdict.

Moreover, if these men testify, the Crown could use their testimony to start a legal action against you for gross indecency.

If we want to avoid this, we must drop your charges against the Marquess at once.

I advise you in your own interest to allow me to make a statement to this effect in court and withdraw from the prosecution. If these men are called, I see your arrest as inevitable.

WILDE: I agree with your advice.

CLARKE: If you wish it I will keep the case going and give you time to get to Calais. There is no necessity for your presence in court while the announcement is being made.

WILDE: No. I shall stay.

NARRATOR 1: Clarke subsequently wrote in his unpublished memoirs of the trial:

CLARKE: I hoped and expected that he would take the opportunity of escaping from the country, and I believe he would have had no difficulty in doing so. The authorities were quite willing that he should go abroad.

NARRATOR 2: Wilde chose to remain in court while Clarke made his statement.

WILDE: I shall stay.

CARSON: The wonder is not that the gossip reached Lord Queensberry, but that, after it was known, this man Wilde should have been tolerated in society in London for the length of time he has.

NARRATOR 3: At this point Sir Edward Clarke was seen to pluck Mr. Carson by the gown. He then interposed and asked leave of the judge to consult with his learned friend. After a few moments of whispered conversation, Mr. Carson returned to his seat.

CLARKE: May I claim your lordship's indulgence while I interpose to make a statement?

JUDGE: Yes you may, Sir Edward.

CLARKE: I think it must be present to your lordship's mind that those who represent Mr. Wilde in this case have before us a very terrible anxiety.

We cannot conceal from ourselves that the evidence that has been submitted might induce the jury to say that Lord Queensberry in using the word "posing" was using a word for which there was sufficient justification.

Under these circumstances, I hope your lordship will think I am taking the right course, which I take after communicating with Mr. Wilde. I feel we could not resist a verdict of not guilty in this case—not guilty having reference to the word "posing."

With this in mind, I now interpose and say on behalf of Mr. Wilde that I would ask to withdraw from the prosecution.

(Audience gasps.)

I trust that this may make an end of the case.

CARSON: I do not know that I have any right whatever to inter-
fere with this application my learned friend has made. I can
only say, as far as Lord Queensberry is concerned, that if
there is a plea of not guilty, this plea must include that his
plea of justification has been proved.

JUDGE: Sir Edward?

*(CLARKE looks at WILDE, who doesn't answer. He then turns to the
JUDGE and assents.)*

JUDGE: I understand him to assent to a verdict of not guilty, and
of course the jury will return that.

CARSON: The verdict will be that the plea of justification has
been proved, and that the words were published for the
public benefit.

CLARKE: Yes, Mr. Carson.

(Three strikes of the gavel)

THE CLERK OF ARRAIGNS: Gentlemen of the jury, do you find the
plea of justification has been proved?

THE FOREMAN OF THE JURY: Yes, we do.

THE CLERK OF ARRAIGNS: And do you find the defendant not
guilty?

THE FOREMAN OF THE JURY: Yes.

THE CLERK OF ARRAIGNS: And that is the verdict of you all?

THE FOREMAN OF THE JURY: Yes.

THE CLERK OF ARRAIGNS: And also that it was published for the public benefit?

THE FOREMAN OF THE JURY: Yes.

CARSON: Of course, the costs of the defense will follow.

JUDGE: Yes.

CARSON: And Lord Queensberry may be discharged.

JUDGE: He may be discharged.

(Three strikes of the gavel)

JUDGE: The court is adjourned.

(Gavel—Applause)

NARRATOR 2: From *The Echo:*

NARRATOR 4: And so a most miserable case is ended. The Marquess of Queensberry is triumphant, and Mr. Oscar Wilde is "damned and done for." He may now change places with the Marquess and go into the dock himself.

NARRATOR 2: Outside the court, prostitutes were dancing on the pavement, lifting their skirts, capering joyfully at the downfall of one whom they regarded as a competitor in trade.

PROSTITUTE: At least he'll have his hair cut reg'lar now!

CLARKE: What a filthy business.

NARRATOR 2: From *Oscar Wilde* by H. Montgomery Hyde:

CLARKE: I shall not feel clean for weeks.

WILDE: What happens now?

CLARKE: We have to wait and see if the Crown will prosecute you.

NARRATOR 2: From *The Daily Telegraph:*

NARRATOR 1: No sterner rebuke could well have been inflicted on some of the artistic tendencies of our time than the condemnation of Oscar Wilde at the Central Criminal Court.

NARRATOR 2: Within minutes of his acquittal, the Marquess of Queensberry dispatched this letter to the Crown's Director of Prosecutions:

QUEENSBERRY: To the Director of Public Prosecutions:
Dear Sir,
    In order that there may be no miscarriage of justice I

think it my duty at once to send you a copy of all our witnesses' statements together with the shorthand notes of the trial.

NARRATOR 2: This step placed the authorities under obligation to act at once.
From *The National Observer:*

NARRATOR 3: There is not a man or woman in the English-speaking world who is not under a debt of gratitude to the Marquess of Queensberry for destroying the high priest of the decadents. This is what art leads to.

NARRATOR 2: On the same day, because of this letter, the Crown decided that a warrant for Wilde's arrest should at once be issued.

NARRATOR 3: From *The National Observer:*
There must be another trial at the Old Bailey, and of the Decadents, of their hideous conceptions of the meaning of Art, there must be an absolute end.

NARRATOR 2: Oscar Wilde was charged with violation of clause 10 of section II of the Criminal Law Amendment Act signed the 1st of January 1885 by Queen Victoria:

QUEEN VICTORIA: Any male person who, in public or in private, commits or is party to the commission of, or procures the commission by any male person of any act of gross indecency with another male person, shall be guilty of a misdemeanor and . . .

SHAW: I appeal now to the champions of individual rights.

NARRATOR 2: George Bernard Shaw on the amendment:

SHAW: There is no justification for that law except the old theological one of making the secular arm the instrument of God's vengeance.

NARRATOR 2: Queen Victoria:

QUEEN VICTORIA: Shall be guilty of a misdemeanor! And, being convicted thereof, shall be liable, at the discretion of the court, to be imprisoned for any term not exceeding two years with or without hard labor.

NARRATOR 2: When asked to sign this bill, Queen Victoria was warned by one of her advisors that:

NARRATOR 3: Mum, the bill does not include similar behavior between women.

NARRATOR 2: To which she responded:

QUEEN VICTORIA: Women don't do such things.

NARRATOR 2: The bill was signed at once. It remained in effect until 1954.

(Three strikes of the gavel)

NARRATOR 1: From court, Oscar Wilde went to the Cadogan Hotel, where Lord Alfred Douglas had taken a room.

There he wrote to *The Evening News*, explaining the reason for his spectacular withdrawal from the case.

WILDE: It would have been impossible for me to have proved my case without putting Lord Alfred Douglas in the witness box against his father. Lord Alfred was extremely anxious to go in the box but I would not let him do so. Rather than place him in so painful a position, I determined to retire from the case, and to bear on my own shoulders whatever ignominy and shame might result from my prosecuting Lord Queensberry.

NARRATOR 3: But nobody really believed this. Robert Sherard's *Life of Oscar Wilde*. At the Cadogan Hotel, Wilde was advised by everyone to go at once to Dover and catch a boat train immediately to Calais.

CLARKE: The authorities were quite willing that he should go abroad.

NARRATOR 1: From Clarke's unpublished memoirs of the trial:

CLARKE: As it was, the warrant was issued only after 5 P.M., to allow him time to catch the last boat train to Calais.

NARRATOR 4: From *Oscar Wilde* by Frank Harris:

HARRIS: At the Cadogan Hotel, Wilde sat as if glued to his chair, and drank hock and seltzer steadily in almost unbroken silence.

QUEENSBERRY: If the country allows you to leave, all the better for the country!

NARRATOR 2: From a note sent to the Cadogan Hotel:

QUEENSBERRY: But if you take my son with you, I will follow you wherever you go and shoot you.

NARRATOR 2: Oscar's wife on hearing of the court's decision said:

CONSTANCE WILDE *(crying):* I hope Oscar is going away abroad!

WILDE: I shall stay and do my sentence whatever that may be.

HARRIS: He then lapsed into inaction.

DOUGLAS: Oscar, I will go to the House of Lords to talk to my cousin. I'll see if he can use his influence to prevent a prosecution.

(He kisses OSCAR *and exits.)*

WILDE: With what a crash this fell.
 I thought but to defend him from his father; I thought of nothing else and now . . .

HARRIS: That was all he said.

NARRATOR 4: At ten past six, two detectives came to the hotel. Wilde went gray in the face. Charles Richards:

RICHARDS: I went with Sergeant Allen to the Cadogan Hotel, and saw the accused there. I said, Mr. Wilde, we are police officers and hold a warrant for your arrest.

WILDE: Yes. Where shall I be taken?

RICHARDS: You will have to go to Scotland Yard with me and then to Bow Street.

WILDE: Can I have bail?

RICHARDS: I don't think you can. I then conveyed Mr. Wilde to Scotland Yard.

NARRATOR 1: Oscar Wilde was imprisoned on the 5th of April, and the trial was set for the 26th of April 1895.

QUEENSBERRY *(Euphoric):* You know, I have not much to do with distinguished people, but I had a very nice letter from Lord Claud Hamilton, and a kind telegram from Mr. Charles Danby, the actor, with "Hearty Congratulations," et cetera. A pile of messages wait for me at *The National Observer* and various clubs have telegraphed also.

(With a pile of messages)
Here's a message: Every man in the city is with you.
Kill the bugger!

End of Act I

ACT II

THE INTERVIEW WITH
MARVIN TAYLOR

MOISES: We have here with us Professor Marvin Taylor, Wilde scholar at New York University, and co-editor of the book *Reading Wilde*.

Mr. Taylor, tell us the thing you find most interesting about the trials.

TAYLOR: Well . . . to me . . . the thing that's most fascinating about the trials is hum. . . . You know . . . there is this real nexus of issues that are on trial with Oscar Wilde and they have to do with the role of art, with effeminacy, with homosexuality, with the Irish in England, with class. . . . So it's not just the fact that Wilde was being tried for sodomy . . . that's not the . . . major point of what's going on. I truly believe that the sodomy charges are really the less important. Wilde was being tried for his subversive beliefs about art, about morality hum . . . about Victorian Society.

You see, Wilde is an aesthete, that is, an artist who argues strenuously for an aesthetic approach, hum . . . and he bases it in Hellenism and in this long tradition of art for art's sake. His project is about art, about the power of art to transform man. Now, as long as he is able to maintain control of the discourse, then he is incredibly you know, hum successful.

MOISES: And what happens in the trial?

TAYLOR: Well, what happens in the trial is he comes head on up against legal discourse, and perhaps I would even say legal-medical discourse. And he begins to lose to this sort of patriarchal medical discourse that makes him appear to be a homosexual, as opposed to . . . hum . . . someone who has desire for other men.

MOISES: Are you saying that Wilde didn't really think of himself as "homosexual"?

TAYLOR: Did Wilde consider himself a kind of person? See, this is what I think is important about the Wilde trials, too, hum. . . . It is *after* the Wilde trials that people began identifying themselves as a specific type of person based on their attraction to people of the same sex. See, it created the modern homosexual as a social subject. Whether Wilde himself thought he was that type of person . . . hum . . . there's nothing in what I know of Greek and Latin literature that says that the Greeks and Romans thought of themselves as homosexuals. So there's nothing necessarily that Wilde would have read that would have made him construct his identity as a homosexual. So it's conceivable that while he loved having sex with men and did, and promoted it through his art even, that he necessarily felt that he was what we would call gay today. I'm not convinced of that. It seems more complicated to me. You know Foucault talks about how it was impossible for men in the Victorian era to think of themselves as gay or homosexual because that construction didn't exist.

MOISES: Well, that leads me to my next question. Why isn't Wilde telling the truth about his desire for men?

TAYLOR: Moisés, this is the thing. Oscar's project was less about sodomy, I think, and more about art, about aestheticism. Wilde was less interested in admitting that he had sex with men than he was interested in expressing his own intellectual ideas, his ideas about beauty and about art.

Though it does look like he lied. I mean we all have that feeling, or we're projecting. Do we want Oscar to be gay therefore we're projecting that he's lying?

Hum, I don't know. But I can see both ways. I worry that we project too much that Oscar was lying. . . .

Then you raise an ethical question.

MOISES: Which is?

TAYLOR: Is it wrong for him to be up on the stand and say that Dorian Gray was a beautiful personality? For him Dorian was a personality. That's what he was attracted to.

MOISES: What do you think is the answer?

TAYLOR: Well, am I to judge him by his own standards or by the standard of the courtroom or by the standard of later gay liberationists. They take him up as a model but inevitably find him unsatisfactory if they pursue it very far because he was about something else.

So, yes he lied but, it doesn't . . . *(chuckle)* . . . I'm on very slippery moral ground here. Ethically it doesn't bother me that he lied. Alas, what they were trying to do I think was to fix homosexuality, to contain the disruption which Wilde presented, and this is a disruption of all kinds of things, of class, of gender, of hum sexuality, hum and they did that, very successfully. But of course by that point he had released these ideas into Western culture that you know . . . are still there.

* * * * * *

NARRATOR 5: From *Oscar Wilde: A Summing Up* by Lord Alfred Douglas:

DOUGLAS: After Oscar's arrest, immediate ruin followed. He had two plays, *An Ideal Husband* and *The Importance of Being Earnest*, running in the West End. He had been up till a week before the trial a comparatively rich man.

Yet the moment he was arrested he was reduced to penury and assailed by all his creditors in a body while all his income simply stopped.

He was of course condemned to pay all my father's costs; the managers suspended the performance of his plays; an execution was put on his house and furniture and effects were sold for a song.

AUCTIONEER: By order of the sheriff, we will auction all the articles in this house, 16 Tite Street, Chelsea.

(Three strikes of the gavel)

The auction will begin with five lots:

A collection of manuscripts of Oscar Wilde's poems.
The original manuscripts of *The Portrait of W. H.*
An autographed copy of *Dorian Gray.*
Oscar Wilde's life length portrait.
A crayon drawing of a nude female by Whistler.

(The AUCTIONEER *continues auctioning the items as* DOUGLAS *proceeds.)*

DOUGLAS: On that day, Wilde's "House Beautiful" presented a pitiful picture: it was overrun by a whole crowd of curiosos, idlers, and rumor mongers. Doors were broken open, valuables were stolen, and the entire sale was carried on amidst scenes of chaotic disorder.

Several original manuscripts mysteriously disappeared and have never since been recovered.

AUCTIONEER: A draft of the play *A Florentine Tragedy.* Do I hear four pounds?

DOUGLAS: From affluence he passed suddenly to dire poverty at a time when money was needed for his defense.

(The sound of the auction grows. DOUGLAS *is forced to raise his voice.)*

Oscar was imprisoned in Holloway Gaol as he waited for another trial.

*(*WILDE *enters escorted by a guard.)*

I used to see him there every day in the ghastly way that visits are arranged in prisons. The prisoner goes into a box rather like the box in a pawn shop. There are rows and rows of these boxes, each occupied by a prisoner and opposite him, the visitor.

AUCTIONEER: Oscar Wilde's life length portrait. I should like to start the bidding for this lot at seven pounds. Do I hear seven pounds . . .

DOUGLAS: We were separated by a corridor about a yard in width and a warder passed up and down between us.

(*Shouting*) We had to shout to make our voices heard above the voices of other prisoners and visitors.

Nothing more revolting and cruel and deliberately malignant could be devised by human ingenuity.

Poor Oscar was rather deaf. He could hardly hear what I said in this tower of Babel. He just looked at me with tears running down his cheeks and I looked at him.

CLARKE: Mr. Justice, my client has been in jail for twenty days. The court date is not set for another ten days. I must once again apply for bail.

JUDGE: There is no worse crime than that with which the prisoner has been charged. I therefore refuse bail.

AUCTIONEER: Sold.

(AUCTIONEER *and* JUDGE *hit their gavels three times in unison. Absolute silence ensues.*)

DOUGLAS: Oscar, I know I always advised you to fight my father, but I am not impervious to reason. If Clarke had assured me that you had no chance, and were merely cutting your own throat and playing into my father's hands, I would have been convinced, Oscar. I never intended for this to happen.

WILDE: The real tragedies in life occur in such an inartistic manner that they hurt us by their crude violence, their absolute incoherence, their absurd want of meaning . . .

(*The guard escorts* WILDE *out.*)

NARRATOR 5: On the day Oscar Wilde was arrested, six hundred gentlemen left England for the continent on a night when usually sixty people traveled. Every train to Dover was crowded, every steamer to Calais thronged with members from the aristocratic and leisured classes.

DOUGLAS: Oscar and his legal advisors urged me to go to France before the second trial. They assured me that my presence in the country could only do Oscar harm. They said that if I were to be called to the witness stand, I should infallibly destroy what small chance he had for acquittal.

His solicitors also told me that unless I left the country, Sir Edward Clarke, who was defending Oscar for no charge, would throw up his defense.

So I embarked for France on the day before the trial, the 25th of April 1895.

It would be two years before I was to see him again.

THE SECOND TRIAL

NARRATOR 5: London, 26th of April 1895, Old Bailey Central Criminal Court, Regina vs. Wilde. Opening speech for the prosecution. Mr. Charles Gill.

(Gavel)

GILL: May it please you, my lord, gentlemen of the jury. This case has received much attention in the press. I must beg you to dismiss from your minds anything you may have heard or read about the prisoner and to abandon all prejudice towards either side, and to approach the case with absolutely open minds, carefully and impartially.

The charge against Mr. Oscar Wilde is that he committed acts of gross indecency with the following male persons: Charles Parker, Frederick Atkins, Sidney Mavor, and Alfred Wood.

NARRATOR 5: Oscar Fingal O'Flahertie Wills Wilde, do you plead guilty or not guilty?

WILDE: I plead not guilty.

NARRATOR 5: George Bernard Shaw on the plea of not guilty:

SHAW: Wilde could plead not guilty with perfect sincerity and indeed could not honestly put in any other plea. Guilty or not guilty is a question not of fact but of morals. The prisoner who pleads not guilty is not alleging that he did this or did not do that; he is affirming that what he did does not involve any guilt on his part.

A man rightly accused of homosexuality is perfectly entitled to plead not guilty in the legal sense. He might admit that he was technically guilty of a breach of local law, and his own conscience might tell him that he was guilty of a sin against the moral law, but if he believes, as Wilde certainly did, that homosexuality is not a crime, he is perfectly entitled to say he is not guilty of it.

GILL: Gentlemen, the prisoner Wilde is well known as a dramatic author and generally as a literary man of unusual attainments. However, we must bear in mind the terrible risks involved in certain artistic and literary phases of the day.

I will begin by reading to the jury the transcripts of the trial of Oscar Wilde vs. the Marquess of Queensberry, specifically, the cross-examination of Wilde on literature, *The Chameleon* and *Dorian Gray.*

CLARKE: My lord, I do not think it fair of Mr. Gill to insist upon reading this. It is not fair to judge a man by his books.

GILL: This is examination as to character.

JUDGE: You may proceed.

GILL: The following is from the transcripts of the first trial: Mr.

Carson asked Mr. Wilde: You are of the opinion, I believe, that there is no such thing as an immoral book?

Mr. Wilde replied: Yes.

Carson: Am I right in saying that you do not consider the effect in creating morality or immorality?

Wilde: In writing a play or a book, I am concerned entirely with literature, that is, with art.

WILDE: Art has a spiritual ministry. It can raise and sanctify everything it touches, and popular disapproval must not impede its progress.

Art is what makes the life of each citizen a sacrament. Art is what makes the life of the whole race immortal.

NARRATOR 5: From *The English Renaissance of Art*:

WILDE: The arts are the only civilizing influences in the world, and without them people are barbarians. An aesthetic education, which humanizes people, is far more important even for politicians than an economic education, which does the opposite.

GILL: Carson asked: Is that good for the young?

Wilde: Anything is good that stimulates thought in any age.

WILDE: Children should not be drilled in that calendar of infamy they call European history, but should learn in a workshop how art might offer a new history of the world, with a promise of the brotherhood of man, of peace rather than war, of praise of God's handymanship, of new imagination and new beauty.

GILL: Carson asked: I take it that no matter how immoral a book might be, if it is well written it would be, in your opinion, a good book?

Wilde: Yes, if it were well written so as to produce a sense of beauty.

WILDE: With the English Renaissance of Art I hoped to create an artistic movement that might change, as it has changed, the face of England.

As time goes on, the men and the forms of expression will change, but the principle remains:

The object of art is to stir the most divine and remote chords which make music in our soul.

Man is hungry for beauty. There is a void.

We spend our days looking for the secret of life. Well, the secret of life is in art.

GILL: Carson asked: Whether moral or immoral?

Wilde: There is no such thing as morality or immorality in thought.

WILDE: I have never come across anyone in whom the moral sense was dominant who was not heartless, cruel, vindictive, log-stupid, and entirely lacking in the smallest sense of humanity. Moral people, as they are termed, are simple beasts. I would sooner have fifty unnatural vices than one unnatural virtue.

The real enemy of modern life, of everything that makes life lovely and joyous and colored for us, is Puritanism, and the Puritan spirit. There is the great danger that lies ahead of the age.

Puritanism is not a theory of life. It is merely an explanation of the English middle classes.

GILL: Carson: Let us go over it phrase by phrase: I quite admit that I adored you madly.

WILDE: Whenever a community or a government of any kind attempts to dictate to the artist what he is to do, art either entirely vanishes or becomes stereotyped, or degenerates into a low and ignoble form of craft. The form of government that is most suitable to the artist is no government at all.

GILL: Carson: Do you mean to say that passage describes the natural feeling of one man towards another?

WILDE: Modern morality consists in accepting the standards of one's age. I consider that for any man of culture to accept the standards of his age is the grossest immorality.

WILDE AND GILL: It would be the influence produced by a beautiful personality.

DOUGLAS: Dear Oscar,
I have just arrived here.

NARRATOR 5: Douglas writes from the Hôtel des Deux Mondes in Paris:

DOUGLAS: They are very nice here, and I can stay as long as I like without paying my bill, which is a good thing as I am quite penniless. The proprietor asked after you at once and expressed his regret and indignation at the treatment you are receiving.
Do keep up your spirit, my dearest darling. I continue

to think of you day and night and send you all my love. I am always your own loving and devoted, Bosie.

GILL: I will now proceed to question the men with whom Mr. Wilde is accused to have committed the acts of gross indecency. I ask you to pay close attention to the testimony of these boys.

(Music—"Rule Britannia" coming from a music box. Four young men enter in Victorian underwear and set up the "shameful den.")

NARRATOR 5: The court calls Charles Parker.

GILL: Please state your age.

PARKER: I am twenty-one years of age.

GILL: Do you have family in London?

PARKER: I have a brother, William.

GILL: What is your occupation?

PARKER: I have been engaged as a valet and my brother as a groom.

GILL: When did you first meet Mr. Alfred Taylor?

PARKER: At the beginning of 1893, I was out of employment. One day I was with my brother at the St. James's Restaurant, in the bar. While there Taylor came up and spoke to us. He was an entire stranger. He passed the compliments of the day and asked us to have a drink. We got into conversation with him. He spoke about men.

GILL: In what way?

PARKER: He called attention to the prostitutes who frequent Piccadilly Circus and remarked, "I can't understand sensible men wasting their money on painted trash like that. Many do, though. But there are a few who know better. Now, you could get money in a certain way easily enough if you cared to." I understood to what Taylor alluded and made a coarse reply.

GILL: I am obliged to ask you what it was you actually said.

PARKER: I do not like to say.

GILL: You were less squeamish at the time, I dare say. I ask you for the words.

PARKER: I said that if any old gentleman with money took a fancy to me, I was agreeable.

(The audience gasps.)

I *was* agreeable. I was terribly hard up.

(Laughter)

GILL: What did Taylor say?

PARKER: Taylor asked us to visit him. He said he could introduce us to a man who was good for plenty of money. If we were interested, we were to meet him (Taylor) at the St. James's bar. We went there the next evening. We were shown upstairs to a private room in which there was a dinner table laid for four. After a while Wilde came in and I was formally introduced. I had never seen him before, but I had heard of him. We dined about eight o'clock. We all four sat down to dinner, Wilde sitting on my left.

GILL: Who made the fourth?

PARKER: My brother, William Parker. I had promised Taylor that he should accompany me.

GILL: Was the dinner a good dinner?

PARKER: Yes. The table was lighted with red-shaded candles. We had plenty of champagne with our dinner and brandy and coffee afterwards. Wilde paid for the dinner.

GILL: What happened after dinner?

PARKER: Wilde said to me, "This is the boy for me! Will you go to the Savoy Hotel with me?" I consented, and Wilde drove me in a cab to the hotel.

GILL: More drink was offered you there?

PARKER: Yes, we had liqueurs. Wilde then asked me to go into his bedroom with him.

GILL: Let us know what occurred there.

MARVIN PARKER: He committed the act of sodomy upon me.

(The court becomes very agitated.)

TAYLOR: From this moment on, Oscar Wilde's name would not be associated with Hellenism or Aestheticism or revolutionary artistic ideals but with homosexuality. He would become the body type, he would become the body type of the invert, of the third sex or whatever. . . . You know. . . . Sociological or medical descriptions for the male homosexual from that period on.

GILL: Did Wilde give you any money that night?

PARKER: Before I left, Wilde gave me £2, telling me to call at the Savoy Hotel in a week. I went there about a week afterwards at eleven o'clock at night. We had supper, with champagne. When I left, he gave me £3.

GILL: What happened at that occasion?

PARKER: I was asked by Wilde to imagine that I was a woman and that he was my lover. I had to keep up this illusion. I used to sit on his knees and he used to . . . as a man might amuse himself with a girl. Wilde insisted on this filthy make-believe being kept up.

GILL: Apart from money, did Wilde give you any presents?

PARKER: Yes, he gave me a silver cigarette case and a gold ring. I don't suppose boys are different to girls in acquiring presents from them who are fond of them.

(Gavel)

NARRATOR 5: The cross-examination of Charles Parker by Sir Edward Clarke:

CLARKE: Did you state at Bow Street that you received £30 from a gentleman to not accuse him of sodomy with you?

PARKER: Yes. I stated at the Police Court that I had received £30, part of monies extorted from a gentleman with whom I had committed acts of indecency. I met the Duke—

CLARKE: I don't ask the name of the gentleman from whom the money was extorted, but I do ask the names of the men who got the money and gave you £30?

PARKER: Alfred Wood and John Allen.

CLARKE: When had the incident occurred in consequence of which you received the £30—how long before?

PARKER: I cannot think.

CLARKE: You had had indecent behavior with the gentleman in question?

PARKER: Yes, but only on one occasion.

CLARKE: Did the gentleman come to your room?

PARKER: Yes.

CLARKE: By your invitation?

PARKER: He asked me if he could come.

CLARKE: And you took him home with you?

PARKER: Yes.

CLARKE: Did Wood and Allen happen to come into the room while the gentleman was there?

PARKER: Yes.

CLARKE: Then they threatened the gentleman with divulging what they had seen?

PARKER: Yes.

CLARKE: How much did Wood and Allen tell you they got?

PARKER: I can't remember.

CLARKE: Try and remember.

PARKER: £300 or £400.

CLARKE: Now, you say positively that Mr. Wilde committed sodomy with you at the Savoy?

PARKER: Yes.

CLARKE: But you have been in the habit of accusing other gentlemen of the same offense?

PARKER: Never, unless it has been done.

CLARKE: I submit that you blackmail gentlemen.

PARKER: No, sir. Wood and Allen did that.

(Laughter in the court)

CLARKE: When Taylor asked you if you ever went with men and got money for it, did you understand what he meant?

PARKER: Yes.

CLARKE: You had heard of such things before?

PARKER: Yes.

CLARKE: You understood the practices you were going to enter upon?

PARKER: Yes.

CLARKE: So you were in no way corrupted by Mr. Wilde.

PARKER *(reluctantly):* No.

CLARKE: Nothing more with this witness.

NARRATOR 5: From *De Profundis:*

WILDE: Why do they jeer at me? I never did them any harm. I never tried to be anything but kind to them.

NARRATOR 5: From a letter from Paris:

DOUGLAS: Oscar, these men are being maintained at Chiswick by the Crown. They have been receiving £5 per week from the beginning of your prosecution of my father until now.

Charles Parker even received a brand new suit of clothes at the Crown's expense.

NARRATOR 5: The Court calls Alfred Wood.

GILL: When did you first meet Alfred Taylor?

WOOD: In January 1893.

GILL: When did you move into his house?

WOOD: In January 1893. I was out of a job and I had nowhere to go.

GILL: How long did you stay there?

WOOD: I lived with him for three weeks.

GILL: Where did you sleep?

WOOD: In the same room with Taylor. There was only one bed there.

GILL: What took place when you were introduced to Wilde?

WOOD: I went to the Café Royal at nine o'clock one evening. Mr. Wilde was sitting down. He spoke to me first. He asked, "Are you Alfred Wood?" I said, "Yes." Then he offered me something to drink and I had something; and then he invited me to go to dinner. I went with him and we dined in a private room.

GILL: What kind of meal was it?

WOOD: Very nice, one of the best to be got.

GILL: What wine did you have?

WOOD: Champagne.

GILL: What happened after dinner?

WOOD: After dinner I went with Mr. Wilde to 16 Tite Street.

GILL: Isn't that where he lives with his wife and two children?

WOOD: Yes. *(Audience gasps.)* But there was nobody in the house, to my knowledge.

NARRATOR 5: From *An Ideal Husband:*

WILDE: People ask me why were you so weak to yield to such temptation. Weak! I am sick of hearing that word. Weak? Do they really think that it is weakness that yields to temptation? I tell you there are terrible temptations that it requires strength, strength and courage to yield to. To stake all one's life on a single moment, to risk everything on one throw, there is no weakness in that. There is a horrible, terrible courage. I had that courage.

WOOD: Mr. Wilde let himself in with a latchkey. We went up to a bedroom, where we had hock and seltzer. There an act of the grossest indecency occurred. Mr. Wilde used his influence to induce me to consent. He made me nearly drunk.

GILL: Did Wilde give you any money that night?

WOOD: Yes, at the Florence. About £3 I think it was.

GILL: Has he given you anything else?

WOOD: He took me out to buy me a present. He bought me half-a-dozen shirts, some collars, and handkerchiefs, and a silver watch and chain.

(Gavel)

NARRATOR 5: The cross-examination of Alfred Wood by Sir Edward Clarke:

CLARKE: Did you go to America?

WOOD: Yes.

CLARKE: When?

WOOD: In 1893.

CLARKE: When did you return?

WOOD: The following year.

CLARKE: What have you been doing since your return from America?

WOOD: Well, I have not done much.

CLARKE: Have you done anything?

WOOD: I have had no regular employment.

CLARKE: I thought not.

WOOD: I could not get anything to do.

CLARKE: As a matter of fact you have had no respectable work for over three years?

WOOD: Well, no.

CLARKE: Charles Parker has told me that you and a man named Allen obtained £300 or £400 from a gentleman whom you blackmailed, and that you gave him £30. Is that true?

WOOD: I didn't get the money. It wasn't paid to me.

CLARKE: Well, tell us, did you get £300 for this blackmail?

WOOD: Not me. Allen did.

CLARKE: You were a party to it?

WOOD: I was there, yes.

CLARKE: Do you mean by that, that you came into the room while the gentleman was there with Parker?

WOOD: I did not; Allen went in first.

CLARKE: At all events Allen and you got £300 to £400 from the gentleman?

WOOD: Yes.

CLARKE: How much did you get?

WOOD: £175.

CLARKE: What for?

WOOD: Well, it was given me by Allen.

CLARKE: Nothing more with this witness.

NARRATOR 5: From *De Profundis:*

WILDE: People thought it dreadful of me to have entertained at dinner these men, and to have found pleasure in their company. But then, from my point of view, they were delightfully suggestive and stimulating. It was like feasting with panthers. They were to me like the brightest of gilded snakes, their poison was part of their perfection. I did not know that when they were to strike at me, it was to be at another's piping and another's pay.

NARRATOR 5: The court calls Fred Atkins.

GILL: How old are you?

ATKINS: I am twenty years old.

GILL: What is your business?

ATKINS: I have been a billiard marker. I have also been a book-maker's clerk and a comedian.

GILL: What do you do?

ATKINS: Currently I'm unemployed.

GILL: Who introduced you to the prisoner?

ATKINS: I was introduced to Mr. Taylor by a young fellow named Schwabe in November 1892. Afterwards Taylor took me to a dinner with Mr. Wilde.

GILL: What happened at the dinner?

ATKINS: Mr. Wilde kissed the waiter.

GILL: Did he ask you to go to Paris with him?

ATKINS: Yes. We were seated at the table, and he put his arm round me and said he liked me. I arranged to meet him two days afterwards at Victoria Station, and went to Paris with him as his private secretary.

GILL: Did any indecencies happen between you and Mr. Wilde in Paris?

ATKINS: No. Once though I got back to the rooms very late. Mr. Wilde was in bed. I went into his room to have myself a drink. A man of about twenty-two years of age was in bed with Mr. Wilde. It was Mr. Schwabe.

The next morning Mr. Wilde came into my room and said to me, "Shall I come into bed with you?" I replied that it was time to get up. Mr. Wilde did not get into bed with me. I returned to London with Mr. Wilde, who gave me money and a silver cigarette case.

(Gavel)

NARRATOR 5: The cross-examination of Fred Atkins by Sir Edward Clarke:

CLARKE: Mr. Atkins, did any impropriety ever take place between you and Mr. Wilde?

ATKINS: Never.

CLARKE: You say Mr. Wilde attempted to come into bed with you.

ATKINS: Yes.

CLARKE: Have you ever been engaged in the business of blackmailing?

ATKINS: I don't remember.

CLARKE: Think!

ATKINS: I never got money in that way.

CLARKE: That being your answer, I must particularize. *(CLARKE shows ATKINS a piece of paper.)* Do you know that name?

ATKINS: No.

CLARKE: On the 9th of June 1891 did you obtain a large sum of money from that gentleman?

ATKINS: Certainly not.

CLARKE: Now I am going to ask you a direct question, and I ask you to be careful in your reply. Were you ever taken to Rochester Row Police Station?

ATKINS: No.

CLARKE: My lord, I wish to call police Constable 396A.

NARRATOR 5: Police Constable 396A is present.

CLARKE: Now I ask you in the presence of this officer, was the statement made at the police station that you and the gentleman had been in bed together?

ATKINS: I don't think so.

CLARKE: Think before you speak. It will be better for you. Did not the landlady actually come into the room and see you and the gentleman naked and in the bed together?

ATKINS: I don't remember that she did.

CLARKE: You may as well tell us about it, you know. I have your statement in my hand. Did not the landlady come into the room at that point?

ATKINS: Well, yes she did.

CLARKE: You had endeavored to force money out of this gentleman?

ATKINS: I asked him for some money.

CLARKE: At the police station the gentleman refused to prosecute?

ATKINS: Yes.

CLARKE: So you were liberated?

ATKINS: Yes.

CLARKE: Atkins, I just asked you these very questions, and you swore upon your oath that you had not been in custody at all, and had never been taken to Rochester Row. How came you to tell me those lies?

ATKINS: I did not remember it.

CLARKE: Nothing more with this witness!

NARRATOR 5: From *De Profundis:*

WILDE: I don't regret for a single moment having lived for pleasure. I did it to the full as one should do anything one does. I wanted to eat of the fruit of all the trees in the garden of the world. I lived on honeycomb!

NARRATOR 5: The Court calls Sidney Mavor.

GILL: Mr. Mavor, how did you meet Mr. Wilde?

MAVOR: One day, Taylor said to me, "I know a man in an influential position who could be of great use to you, Mavor. He likes young men when they're modest and nice in appearance. I'll introduce you."

It was arranged that we should dine at Kettner's Restaurant the next evening. When I got there, Taylor said, "I'm glad you've made yourself pretty. Mr. Wilde likes nice clean boys." That was the first time Wilde's name was mentioned.

GILL: What happened next?

MAVOR: On our arrival at the restaurant we were shown into a private room. Wilde came in with another gentleman. I believe the other gentleman was Lord Alfred Douglas.

NARRATOR 5: From *The Autobiography of Lord Alfred Douglas:*

DOUGLAS: Before I left for Paris I happened to see Mavor at the Bow Street Police Court, while he was waiting to give evidence.

Mavor was a gentleman by birth and of an entire different character and class than the other witnesses. He was being terrorized into making a statement by the same means as the other so-called "witnesses."

MAVOR: I was placed next to Wilde, who used occasionally to pull my ear or chuck me under the chin, but he did nothing that was actually objectionable. Wilde said to Taylor, "Our little lad has pleasing manners. We must see more of him." Wilde took my address, and soon afterwards I received a silver cigarette case with my Christian name scratched inside it. It was inscribed "Sidney from O. W., October, 1892."

DOUGLAS: I went up to him and shook hands and said: Sidney, surely you are not going to give evidence against Oscar?

MAVOR: Soon after, I received a letter from Mr. Wilde making an appointment to meet him at the Albemarle Hotel. I arrived at the hotel soon after eight, and we had supper in a private room. I subsequently stayed the night.

DOUGLAS: Sidney!

MAVOR: Well, what can I do? I daren't refuse to give evidence now; they got a statement out of me.

DOUGLAS: For God's sake, Sidney, remember you are a gentleman and a public school boy. Don't put yourself on a level with Parker and Atkins. When counsel asks you questions, deny the whole thing and say you were frightened by the police. They can't do anything to you.

GILL: Did any misconduct take place that night?

MAVOR: No. No misconduct ever took place between Mr. Wilde and me.

GILL: Mr. Mavor, I repeat the question: Did any misconduct take place that night?

MAVOR: No. No misconduct ever took place between Mr. Wilde and me.

DOUGLAS: Counsel of course dropped him like a hot brick!

GILL: Nothing more with this witness.

(Gavel)

NARRATOR 5: The cross-examination of Sidney Mavor by Sir Edward Clarke:

CLARKE: Did any impropriety ever take place between you and Mr. Wilde?

MAVOR: No, never.

CLARKE: Has Mr. Wilde ever given you any money?

MAVOR: No. I was glad of Mr. Wilde's friendship.

CLARKE: Thank you. No more questions, my lord.

GILL: That is the case for the Crown, my lord.

(Blackout)

NARRATOR 5: Second trial. Fourth day—Tuesday, 30th of April 1895.
 The opening speech for the defense, Sir Edward Clarke:

CLARKE: This trial seems to be operating as an act of indemnity for all the blackmailers in London. In testifying on behalf of the Crown they have received immunity for past rogueries and indecencies, these men who ought to be the accused, not the accusers.
 You must not act upon suspicion or prejudice, but

upon examination of the facts, gentlemen, and on the facts, I respectfully urge that Mr. Wilde is entitled to claim from you a verdict of acquittal.

It was Mr. Wilde's act, and Mr. Wilde's act alone, in charging Lord Queensberry with libel which has brought the matter before the public and placed him in his present position of peril.

Men who have been charged with the offenses alleged against Mr. Wilde shrink from investigation. Mr. Wilde taking the initiative of a public trial is evidence of his innocence. Nor is that all. A few days before the first trial, notice was given of certain charges made against him with the names of these young men. Mr. Wilde knew the catalogue of accusations. Gentlemen of the jury, do you believe that had he been guilty he would have stayed in England and faced those accusations? What would you think of a man who, knowing himself to be guilty and that evidence would be forthcoming from half-a-dozen different places, insisted on bringing his case before the world? Insane would hardly be the word for it if Mr. Wilde really had been guilty and yet faced that investigation.

NARRATOR 5: The examination of Oscar Wilde by Sir Edward Clarke:

CLARKE: With reference to the Queensberry trial, was the evidence you gave on that occasion absolutely and in all respects true?

WILDE: Entirely true evidence.

CLARKE: And what part of what these youths have said is true?

WILDE: I have been acquainted with all of them, but nothing ever happened with any one of them.

CLARKE: Of what Charles Parker said, what is untrue?

WILDE: Where he says he came to the Savoy Hotel and that I committed acts of indecency with him. He never went to the Savoy with me to supper. It is true that he dined with me. The rest is untrue.

CLARKE: Alfred Wood.

WILDE: It is entirely untrue that he ever went to Tite Street with me at all.

CLARKE: Fred Atkins.

WILDE: It is not true when he says he came into my room and saw me with Mr. Schwabe in bed. Mr. Schwabe was in Paris, and it is true that Atkins slept in the room he described next to mine.

CLARKE: Why did you ask Sidney Mavor to spend the night with you at the Albermarle?

WILDE: As company for me and a compliment for himself.

NARRATOR 5: From *Oscar Wilde: A Summing Up* by Lord Alfred Douglas:

DOUGLAS: It would have been infinitely better if Oscar had told the truth. Of course, everyone would have told him that to do so would be utterly fatal. But if he had had the courage to do it, he stood a chance of striking a blow for justice by telling the truth and saying what he really thought and passionately believed.

NARRATOR 5: The cross-examination of Oscar Wilde by Mr. Charles Gill:

GILL: Mr. Wilde, why did you take up with these youths?

WILDE: I am a lover of youth.

(Laughter)

GILL: You exalt youth as a sort of god?

WILDE: I like to study the young in everything. There is something fascinating in youthfulness.

GILL: How old was Lord Alfred Douglas when you met him?

WILDE: Twenty years old.

GILL: Did Lord Alfred Douglas contribute some verses to *The Chameleon*?

WILDE: Yes.

GILL: The poems in question were somewhat peculiar?

WILDE: They certainly were not mere commonplaces like so much that is labeled poetry.

GILL: You described them as beautiful poems?

WILDE: I said something tantamount to that. The verses were original in theme and construction, and I admired them.

GILL: The following poem is called "Two Loves." In it, two boys meet. One boy says:

"I am true Love, I fill
The hearts of boy and girl with mutual flame.

Then sighing, the other says, 'Have thy will,
I am the Love that dare not speak its name.'"

Was that poem explained to you?

WILDE: I think it is clear.

GILL: There is no question as to what it means?

WILDE: Most certainly not.

GILL: Is it not clear that the love described relates to natural love and unnatural love?

WILDE: No.

GILL: What is the "Love that dare not speak its name"?

WILDE: The "Love that dare not speak its name" in this century is such a great affection of an elder for a younger man as there was between David and Jonathan, such as Plato made the very basis of his philosophy, and such as you find in the sonnets of Michelangelo and Shakespeare. It is that deep, spiritual affection that is as pure as it is perfect. It dictates and pervades great works of art like those of Shakespeare and Michelangelo, and those two letters of mine, such as they are. It is in this century misunderstood, so much misunderstood that it may be described as the "Love that dare not speak its name," and on account of it I am placed where I am now. It is beautiful, it is fine, it is the noblest form of affection. There is nothing unnatural about it. It is intellectual, and it repeatedly exists between an elder and a younger man when the elder man has intellect and the younger man has all the joy, hope, and glamour of life before him. That it should be so the world does not understand. The world mocks at it and sometimes puts one in the pillory for it.

(Loud applause, mingled with some hisses.)

JUDGE: Order! *(Three strikes of the gavel)* Order! *(Three strikes of the gavel)* Order! *(Three strikes of the gavel)* If there is the slightest manifestation of feeling I shall have the court cleared. Complete silence must be preserved.

GILL: With regard to your friendship towards the men who have given evidence, may I take it that it was, as you describe, Mr. Wilde, a deep affection of an elder man for a younger?

WILDE: Certainly not! One feels that once in one's life, and once only, towards anybody.

NARRATOR 5: From *The Autobiography of Lord Alfred Douglas:*

DOUGLAS: I am proud to have been loved by a great poet. There will always be one thousand Queensberrys for one Oscar Wilde.

GILL: Nothing more with this witness.

(Three strikes of the gavel)

JUDGE: Gentlemen of the jury, I have received a communication from you to the effect that you are unable to arrive at an agreement.

THE FOREMAN OF THE JURY: That is so, my lord. We cannot agree.

JUDGE: Is there any prospect that if you retired to your room and continued your deliberations for a while longer you would be able to come to an agreement?

THE FOREMAN OF THE JURY: I put that also to my fellow-jurymen. We have considered the question for three hours, and we cannot agree.

JUDGE: That being so, I do not feel justified in detaining you any longer. The prisoner will be held in prison until further notice. I will see counsel in my chambers to set the date for the next trial. This court is adjourned!

(Three strikes of the gavel)

NARRATOR 5: Sir Edward Clarke applied for bail and it was refused by the trial judge.

Wilde was imprisoned again.

Four days later, Clarke applied again and bail was granted, by another judge, in the extortionate sum of £5,000.

From *Oscar Wilde* by Sheridan Morley:

Wilde went to the Midland Hotel and dinner was ordered. No sooner had he sat down than the hotel manager came in and said:

HOTEL MANAGER: You are Oscar Wilde, I believe.

WILDE: Yes.

HOTEL MANAGER: You must leave this hotel at once!

NARRATOR 5: From this hotel he went to another on the outskirts of London. He sank down exhausted on the bed of the room. The landlord appeared.

LANDLORD: Sir, I am sorry, but you have been followed by a band of prize-fighters. They say they will sack the house and raze the street if you stay here a moment longer. I must insist that you leave.

NARRATOR 5: At last, after midnight, he arrived at his mother's house in Oakley Street.

WILDE: Give me shelter, Willie. Let me lie on the floor or I shall die in the streets.

WILLIE: Come in.

NARRATOR 5: His brother Willie:

WILLIE *(drunk):* Thank God my vices are decent.

NARRATOR 5: Frank Harris came to see him in Oakley Street the following morning.

WILDE: I feel that public disgrace is in store for me, I feel certain of it. I never knew what terror was before. I know it now. It is as if a hand of ice were laid upon one's heart. It's as if one's heart were beating itself to death in some empty hollow.

HARRIS: Oscar, I have a yacht waiting to take you to France. You must go!

WILDE: I can't, Frank, I can't.

HARRIS: Listen, Oscar. I will not cross my arms and let that band of crooks get the best of you.

WILDE: Oh, Frank, you talk with passion and conviction, as if I were innocent.

HARRIS: But you are innocent, aren't you?

WILDE: No, Frank. I thought you knew that all along.

HARRIS: No. I did not know. I did not believe the accusation. I did not believe it for a moment. I thought that men confuse the artistic nature with that vice but . . .

WILDE: What you call vice, Frank, is not vice. It is good to me. This will make a great difference to you, Frank?

HARRIS: No. Curiously enough it has made no difference to me at all. I do not know why; I suppose I have got more sympathy than morality in me. It has surprised me, dumbfounded me. The thing has always seemed fantastic and incredible to me. And now you make it exist for me. But it has no effect on my friendship, none upon my resolve to help you.

WILDE: You have been a good friend to me, a thoroughly good friend.

HARRIS: I don't know I have been able to do much for you. In fact, I have not been able to do anything for you, as I can see. I am thoroughly disappointed with myself.

WILDE: You have enabled me to tell you the truth, that is something. To speak the truth is a painful thing. To be forced to tell lies is much worse.

HARRIS: Well, now I must take you away immediately.

WILDE: Oh, that would be wonderful, Frank, but it's impossible. Quite impossible. I should be arrested before I left London, and shamed again in public. They would boo at me and shout insults. Oh! It is impossible. I could not risk it.

HARRIS: Nonsense! I believe the authorities would be only too glad if you went.

WILDE: And what about the people who have stood bail for me? I couldn't leave them to suffer. They would lose their thousands.

HARRIS: I shan't let them lose. I'm quite willing to take half on my shoulders at once. And you can pay the other thousand or so within a very short time by writing a couple of plays. American papers would be only too glad to pay you for an interview. The story of your escape would be worth a thousand pounds. They would give you almost any price for it. Leave everything to me.

NARRATOR 5: Wilde's family had other opinions. His brother:

WILLIE *(drunk):* You are an Irishman. You must stay and face the music.

NARRATOR 5: His mother:

SPERANZA: If you stay, no matter what happens, you will always be my son. If you leave, I shall never talk to you again.

NARRATOR 5: His wife:

CONSTANCE WILDE: You must go, Oscar.

NARRATOR 5: A letter from Oscar Wilde to Bosie on the evening of his third trial:

WILDE: I have decided that it is nobler and more beautiful to stay. We cannot be together. I do not want to be called a coward or a deserter. A false name, a disguise, a hunted life, all that is not for me. Oh sweetest of all boys, most loved of all loves, my soul clings to your soul, my life to your life, and in all the worlds of pain and pleasure you are my ideal of admiration and joy.

NARRATOR 5: From *The Autobiography of Lord Alfred Douglas:*

DOUGLAS: I don't like to think of it, but I have thought since a hundred times that it was an insane thing not to go, and that really leaving would have been a braver thing to do.

NARRATOR 4: An official announcement: The next trial will not be led by Mr. Gill. The Crown is naming Frank Lockwood, the Solicitor-General, as the prosecution attorney.

NARRATOR 1: From a letter sent by Douglas to the French magazine *Mercure de France:*

DOUGLAS: The third trial is a result of a political intrigue. The government does not wish to let the prosecution of Oscar Wilde take its regular course.

NARRATOR 2: From *Oscar Wilde* by H. Montgomery Hyde: Carson, who had refused to be the Crown's prosecutor against Wilde, now went to Lockwood and said:

CARSON: Cannot you let up on the fellow now? The jury was deadlocked, Frank.

LOCKWOOD: I would, but we cannot, we dare not. It would at once be said both in England and abroad that, owing to the nature of this case, we were forced to abandon it.

DOUGLAS: The government is intimidated. The fact is that the liberal party presently contains a large number of men that have the same inclinations as Wilde does. People are talking about them. To hush up these rumors, Oscar must be found guilty.

CARSON: Wilde has suffered a great deal. In addition, he has already spent over a month in prison, with no possibility of bail, just awaiting a trial.

DOUGLAS: I would wish to ask the Home Secretary this: Is it not true that you have been threatened by the Prime Minister that if a second trial was not instituted and a verdict of guilty obtained against Mr. Wilde, the liberal party would be removed from power?

LOCKWOOD: I can't, Edward. It would be seen as an act of weakness. Besides, many people in this government are said to be implicated in similar affairs. It would be said that it is because of those people that we are forced to abandon the case. We must go on till the end.

DOUGLAS: It is a degrading coup d'état—the sacrifice of a great poet to save a degraded band of politicians.

NARRATOR 1: The *Mercure de France* refused to publish Douglas's letter.

THE THIRD TRIAL

NARRATOR 4: The third trial, Old Bailey Central Criminal Court, Regina vs. Wilde.

LOCKWOOD: I am bound to assume that, as you are an entirely fresh jury, you are totally ignorant of all the facts which have been elucidated in the previous trial of the prisoner. It will, therefore, be necessary to go through the entire case again in detail.

(WILDE *reacts. He is exhausted, desperate.*)

(*During this segment, the sound of a heartbeat can be heard, in a gradual crescendo, until Wilde's speech ending in "If hatred gives you pleasure, indulge it."*)

The defendant is charged with having committed offenses under section 2 of the Criminal Law Amendment Act of 1885: Gross indecency with male persons. He has repeatedly used his influence to corrupt young men of quite inferior station. He led these men into the most vicious and depraved conduct. . . .

NARRATOR 5: From *De Profundis:*

WILDE: I remember when I was sitting in the dock on my last trial, listening to Lockwood's appalling denunciation of me—like a thing out of Tacitus, like a passage in Dante—and being sickened with horror at what I heard.

LOCKWOOD: That Wilde has been at the center of a circle of hideous corruption among young men it is impossible to doubt . . .

PARKER: My name is Charles Parker, I'm twenty-one years of age. Mr. Wilde committed sodomy with me on . . .

WILDE: I must say to myself that I ruined myself, and that nobody great or small can be ruined except by their own hand. This pitiless indictment I bring without pity against myself. I let myself be lured into long spells of senseless and sensual ease.

WOOD: My name is Alfred Wood, I'm twenty-two years old, Mr. Wilde . . .

WILDE: I surrounded myself with the smaller natures and the meaner minds. I became the spendthrift of my genius. I grew careless of the lives of others. I took pleasure where it pleased me and passed on.

ATKINS: My name is Fred Atkins, I am twenty years old. Three times Mr. Wilde . . .

WILDE: I forgot that every little action of the common day makes or unmakes character, and that therefore what one does in the secret chamber one has some day to cry aloud on the housetops.

LOCKWOOD: The Crown will present witnesses that will on oath state that . . .

WILLIAM PARKER: I am the brother of Charles Parker. My brother accepted a preserved cherry from Wilde's own mouth.

WILDE: I blame myself terribly. As I sit here, a ruined man, it is myself I blame.

MRS. ELLEN GRANT: I am the landlady. The windows were never opened or cleaned, and the daylight was never admitted.

WILDE: While there is nothing wrong in what I did, there is something wrong in what I became.

THOMAS PRICE: I am a waiter at a private hotel at 10 St. James's Place. A number of young men of quite inferior station called there to see Wilde.

WILDE: How weary I am of the whole thing, of the shame and the struggling and the hatred. To see those people coming into the box one after the other to witness against me makes me sick.

GEORGE FREDERICK CLARIDGE: I am a silversmith. I supplied Mr. Wilde with silver cigarette cases.

WILDE: Reason does not help me. It tells me that the law under which I'm being judged is a wrong and unfair law, and the system under which I'm suffering, a wrong and unjust system.

MARY APPLEGATE: I am the housekeeper. After Mr. Wilde's visit, the sheets were stained in a peculiar way.

WILDE: The world is growing more tolerant. One day you will be ashamed of your treatment of me.

ANTONIO MIGGE: I am professor of massage. Once I saw a young man in bed with Mr. Wilde. I never attended Mr. Wilde again.

WILDE: I feel inclined to stretch out my hands and cry to them: Do what you will with me, in God's name, only do it quickly. Can you not see I'm worn out? If hatred gives you pleasure, indulge it.

(Silence)

LOCKWOOD: When did your acquaintance with Lord Alfred Douglas begin?

WILDE: In 1892.

LOCKWOOD: And when did the Marquess of Queensberry first object?

WILDE: In April 1894.

(WILDE is exhausted.)

LOCKWOOD: Mr. Wilde, where is Lord Alfred Douglas now?

WILDE: He is abroad.

LOCKWOOD: Where?

WILDE: In Paris, at the Hôtel des Deux Mondes.

LOCKWOOD: Of course you have been in communication with him.

WILDE: Certainly. These charges are founded on sand. Our friendship is founded on a rock. There has been no need to cancel the acquaintance.

LOCKWOOD: This is from the now notorious prose-poem you wrote to Lord Alfred Douglas: "My own dear boy, Your sonnet is quite lovely."
  Why did you choose the words "My own dear boy"?

WILDE: My dearest boy,

NARRATOR 5: A letter from Oscar Wilde to Lord Alfred Douglas written on the final night of the trials from Holloway Prison:

WILDE: This is to assure you of my immortal, my eternal love for you. Tomorrow all will be over.

DOUGLAS (reading): If prison and dishonor be my destiny, think that my love for you and this idea, this still more divine belief that you love me in return will sustain me in my unhappiness and will make me capable, I hope, of bearing my grief most patiently.

WILDE: Since the hope, nay rather the certainty, of meeting you again in some world is the goal and the encouragement of my present life, I must continue to live in this world because of that.

LOCKWOOD: Was it a decent way to address a young man?

WILDE: I am so happy that you've gone away! I know what that must have cost you. It would have been agony for me to think that you were in England when your name was mentioned in court.

LOCKWOOD: Were you speaking of love between men?

WILDE: I hope you have copies of all my books. All mine have been sold. I stretch out my hands toward you. Oh! That I may live to touch your hair and your hands. I feel certain that your love will watch over my life. Try to let me hear from you soon.

LOCKWOOD: Was it sensual love?

WILDE: I am writing you this letter in the midst of great suffering—this long day in court has exhausted me.
    Dearest boy, sweetest of all young men, most loved and most lovable: Wait for me!

DOUGLAS *(Reading):* Wait for me! I am now, as ever since the day we met, yours devoutly and with an immortal love,

WILDE and DOUGLAS: Oscar.

LOCKWOOD: What was the charge which Lord Queensberry made against you?

WILDE *(shouting):* Posing sodomite.

(Three strikes of the gavel. The actors move about the stage in a fury.)

NARRATOR 3: Gentlemen of the jury, this case is a most difficult one and my task very severe.

NARRATOR 4: I would rather try the most shocking murder case that has ever fallen to my lot to try than be engaged in a case of this description.

NARRATOR 1: It is a case which, notwithstanding the horrible nature of the charges involved, calls for the cold, calm, resolute administration of justice.

NARRATOR 2: Oscar Wilde is an artist who exercised considerable influence over young men.

NARRATOR 6: He has used his art to subvert morality

NARRATORS 4 AND 6: and to encourage unnatural vice.

WILDE: I was a man who stood in symbolic relation to the art and culture of my age. Few men hold such a position in their own lifetime and have it so acknowledged.

I had genius, a distinguished name, high social position, brilliancy, intellectual daring. I made art a philosophy, and philosophy an art. I altered the minds of men and the colors of things. There was nothing I said or did that did not make people wonder. Whatever I touched I made beautiful in a new mode of beauty. I treated art as the supreme reality and life as a mere mode of fiction. I awoke the imagination of my century so that it created myth and legend around me. I summed up all systems in a phrase, and all existence in an epigram.

(Three strikes of the gavel)

THE CLERK OF ARRAIGNS: Gentlemen, have you agreed upon a verdict?

THE FOREMAN OF THE JURY: Yes, we have.

THE CLERK OF ARRAIGNS: Do you find the prisoner at the bar guilty or not guilty of acts of gross indecency?

THE FOREMAN OF THE JURY: We find him guilty, my lord.

JUDGE: Oscar Wilde, the crime of which you have been convicted is so bad that one has to put a firm restraint upon oneself to prevent oneself from describing, in terms I would rather not use, the sentiments which must rise to the breast of every man of honor who has heard the details of these terrible three trials.

It is no use for me to address you. People who can do these things are dead to all sense of shame, and one cannot hope to produce any effect upon them.

This is the worst case I have ever tried.

I shall, under such circumstances, be expected to pass the severest sentence allowed by the law. It is in my opinion, totally inadequate for such a case as this.

The sentence of the court is that you be imprisoned and kept to hard labor for two years.

(Cries of oh! oh! and Shame!)

WILDE: And I? May I say nothing, my lord?

NARRATOR 2: His lordship made no reply beyond a wave of the hand to the warders, who hurried the prisoner out of sight.

(WILDE *exits.*)

JUDGE: The jury is discharged. The court is adjourned.

(Three strikes of the gavel)

EPILOGUE

NARRATOR 4: The press lived up to Wilde's expectation by almost universally praising the verdict. *The Daily Telegraph:*

NARRATOR 1: Open the windows! Let in the fresh air!

NARRATOR 4: *The News of the World:*

NARRATOR 2: The Aesthetic Cult is over!

NARRATOR 4: *The St. James Gazette:*

NARRATOR 3: A dash of wholesome bigotry is better than over-toleration!

ACTOR PLAYING LORD ALFRED DOUGLAS: Oscar Wilde spent the next two years in prison. During this time, his wife changed her name and the name of their children. He also fell in his cell and injured his ear. In prison this injury was not properly treated and was to deteriorate and be the cause of his death three years later.

During his time in prison, Wilde turned against Lord Alfred Douglas. He blamed him for his downfall.

He wrote there the "The Ballad of Reading Gaol," which contains the line "for each man kills the things he loves." Lord Alfred Douglas asked him what he meant by this and Wilde said, "You ought to know."

NARRATOR 2: After his release from prison, Wilde and Douglas lived together on and off until Wilde's death in 1900.

NARRATOR 4: After Wilde's death Lord Alfred Douglas married and had two children. He became a Catholic, and eventually a Nazi sympathizer.

NARRATOR 3: The Marquess of Queensberry died in 1899, a pathetic victim of persecution mania, convinced to the last that he was being harried to the tomb by "Oscar Wilders," as he used to describe his imaginary tormentors.

NARRATOR 4: Oscar Wilde was buried at Bagneux Cemetery on the 3rd of December 1900. Lord Alfred Douglas was one of the twelve people who attended the burial.

NARRATOR 1: By the year 1920, Oscar Wilde was, after Shakespeare, the most widely read English author in Europe.

CODA

NARRATOR 1: This is from a prose poem written by Oscar Wilde a year after his release from prison. It's called "The House of Judgment."

NARRATOR 5: And there was silence in the House of Judgment. And the Man came naked before God.
    And God opened the Book of the Life of the Man.
    And God said to the Man:

NARRATOR 4: Thy life hath been evil, and thou hast shown cruelty to those who were in need of succor, and to those who lacked help thou hast been bitter and hard of heart.

NARRATOR 7: The poor called to thee and thou didst not hearken, and thine ears were closed to the cry of My afflicted.

NARRATOR 5: And the Man made answer and said:

NARRATOR 1: Even so did I.

NARRATOR 5: And again God opened the Book of the Life of the Man.
    And God said to the Man:

NARRATOR 6: Thou didst eat of the thing that may not be eaten. Thine idols were neither of gold nor of silver that endure, but of flesh that dieth.

NARRATOR 3: Thou didst stain their hair with perfumes and put pomegranates in their hands.

NARRATOR 8: Thou didst stain their feet with saffron and spread carpets before them.

NARRATOR 5: And the Man made answer and said:

NARRATOR 1: Even so did I.

NARRATOR 5: And a third time God opened the Book of the Life of the Man.
     And God said to the Man:

NARRATOR 2: Evil hath been thy life, and with evil didst thou requite good, and with wrongdoing kindness.

NARRATOR 6: He who came to thee with water went away thirsting.

NARRATOR 7: And to those who brought thee Love thou didst ever give Lust in thy turn.

NARRATOR 5: And the Man made answer and said:

NARRATOR 1: Even so did I.

NARRATOR 5: And God closed the Book of the Life of the Man, and said:

NARRATOR 8: Surely I will send thee into Hell. Even into Hell will I send thee.

NARRATOR 5: And the Man cried out:

NARRATOR 1: Thou canst not.

NARRATOR 5: And God said to the Man:

NARRATOR 2: Wherefore can I not send thee to Hell, and for what reason?

NARRATOR 1: Because in Hell I have always lived,

NARRATOR 5: Answered the Man.
And there was silence in the House of Judgment.
And after a space God spake, and said to the Man:

NARRATOR 7: Then surely I will send thee unto Heaven. Even unto Heaven will I send thee.

NARRATOR 5: And the Man cried out:

NARRATOR 1: Thou canst not.

NARRATOR 5: And God said to the Man:

NARRATOR 6: Wherefore can I not send thee unto Heaven, and for what reason?

NARRATOR 1: Because never, and in no place, have I been able to imagine it,

NARRATOR 5: Answered the Man.
And there was silence in the House of Judgment.

End of Play

AFTERWORD

BY TONY KUSHNER

Every once in a while the beleaguered human race refreshes itself by producing a new artist, scientist, philosopher, or even, on very rare occasion, a genuinely gifted politician. New talent (what the antivocational Oscar Wilde would have called a fascinating personality)—at its first appearance, usually as a sudden bright nova of annunciation to that majority of admirers which has been spared its slow, painful development—causes all the other stars in the sky to appear to shift position, to dull or brighten or revolve in relation to it; it enlivens and makes interesting again the whole familiar firmament, which feat adds to the luster of its specific accomplishment. Except for changing, even the gaudy heavens would grow dull.

I'd heard of Moisés Kaufman, that he was a talented director, at some point before his recent success. Within days of *Gross Indecency*'s flaring the horizon, I was hearing about very little else. It was obvious that something truly important had happened, because the play was exciting not only the professionally and habitually overly excitable (about 75 percent of the population of the New York art world), but the professionally and habitually sobersided and ungenerous as well, and people with good taste—whose number corresponds nearly exactly with that small percentage of the population in frequent agreement with me.

Nearly everyone who has seen it speaks of *Gross Indecency* in tones of exhilaration and relief; when something actually deserving of success is rewarded rather than punished, we all breathe easier. The world seems a more just place (a dangerous illusion, but we are entitled to our dangerous illusions every now and again). The human community seems not to have lost all its marbles (displacing the equally dangerous illusion that it has lost them). And, again, the earth appears younger, or at any rate less exhausted, by the incipiency of a new stellation: "the way a single light in the evening sky in spring," writes Wallace Stevens, "creates a fresh universe out of nothingness by adding itself."

I hope it's okay that I'm beginning by discussing Moisés Kaufman rather than his play or his play's subject, about whom so much has been written, so many opinions formed and delivered, who is introduced and illuminated so magnificently in the text you have just read. Oscar is in Elysium now, no one can hurt him there. He is dead, and a darling of all sorts of people, gay and straight. He is a real hero of social progress, and one of the best things about *Gross Indecency* is that it emphasizes, with marvelous subtlety, Wilde's heart-stopping courage, stripped in the process of dramatization of none of its complexity or even pathology—which Wilde has shared with all other examples of courage and bravery, for who wants to be destroyed? Homosexual liberationists and advocates of free speech and thought are wild for Wilde; we paint him on our banners. Weirdly (or, perhaps, alarmingly, not so weirdly), even right-wing critic-elegists like Yale Kramer adore Oscar, as an early prophet of antigovernment, as one who laughs in the face of compassion, as a thorny old individualist, the Belle Epoque's answer to P. J. O'Rourke, and, of course, as a member in good standing of the ivied Academy against which the grungy present can be unfavorably compared and dismissed (by people who would have bayed like bloodhounds throughout the Wilde trials).

Wilde's antigovernment anarchism meant something very different in the 1880s and '90s than it does in the 1980s and '90s. All anarchisms, even ego-anarchism, a hundred years ago were politically positioned to the left; this is no longer the case. Wilde's shares with all anarchisms both an inescapable truth, that where there is law there is no freedom (in the absolute sense—and anarchism is always absolute), and an unavoidable silliness. Anarchism has recently become a conventicle for some rather seedy types. When Oscar opines, as you will read him doing in the text of the play, that the only good government for artists is no government at all, I hope you will hear Newt Gingrich grunting his approval as he demolishes the NEA, see in your peripheral vision Reagan's head nodding in nostalgio-sclerotic agreement. Maybe, if you, like me, are a bit of a hysteric, you will see the gigantic plumes of concrete dust rising from the bombed Federal Office Building in Oklahoma City! "Self-sacrifice is a thing that should be put down by the law. It is so demoralizing to the people for whom one sacrifices oneself." Didn't I just read that in the Contract With America? Or was it in some co-dependency twelve-step brochure? "If the poor only had profiles there would be no difficulty solving the problem of poverty." Well, one sees Oscar's point, one nervously supposes.

That nervousness is salutary, of course. All dialetics (and Wilde is nothing if not dialectical, though more in the Jesuitical sense than in the Hegelian) should produce a bad case of the jitters; if not, you're not trying hard enough. And anyone, right or left, would be a fool to not prefer either of the above salty apothegms to Bill "Bipartisan Compromise" Clinton's husky assurances that he "feels our pain" while preparing to sign the Welfare Reform Act.

Moisés Kaufman's character "Marvin Taylor" (and how nice for Marvin to have been turned into a dramatis persona!)

explores the political potency of the Wildean paradox brilliantly in the play. Mr. Taylor speaks here for writers and critics like Michel Foucault, Alan Sinfield, Ed Cohen, Jonathan Dollimore, and the whole splendid Queer Theoretical Company, who have made it clear that our Oscar was an aesthete but no wilting wimp. Charm, which Evelyn Waugh famously identified as the dry-rot infecting the English soul, was transformed by Wilde into something vivid—almost too vivid—subversive, magical, undeniably politically irruptive, and effective. Wilde charmed history. His charm has less to do with good manners and a pleasant demeanor than with what postmodern physicists speak about when they speak of subatomic "charm": an elusive but fundamental valence, a force profoundly influencing the structure of things.

On the other hand: One of *Gross Indecency*'s other heroes is George Bernard Shaw, who got so much so right so impressively early on. A dialectician conversant with the theoretical literature of a progressive movement (in Shaw's case, socialism) and possessed of a materialist belief in the importance of the political economy, Shaw achieves as observer of the course of Wilde's trials a kind of prescient, almost prophetic clarity. There are advantages to grounding one's iconoclasm in antecedence, in the historical continuum. There are advantages in not striving too feverishly, as Wilde did, for originality-for-its-own-sake, and in the process subsuming a thousand years of human struggle into a Grand Ineffable Whatsist called "Art."

This is not to say that the Grand Ineffable Whatsist wasn't utterly magnificent, wasn't political. But it was ahistorical, or so it pretended (posed); it forsook the continuum of history and leapt for antecedence back to quasi-mythologized antiquities. Wilde called himself a socialist, and I believe he was. But his was an anarcho-socialism, mortgaged heavily to nonsocialist essentialisms like the Eternal and the Beautiful. Wilde's socialism is too easily packed away, out of sight, while the anarchism and essentialism glitters dangerously forth. Or so it seems to me. I believe in narrative. I am, I suppose, a rationalist. Wilde can't be the patron saint of people like me—besides being, possibly, "mildly" anti-Semitic, he goes on too much about Beauty, and I'm not beautiful and I don't know what he means. W. B. Yeats, comparing Shaw to Wilde, accuses the former of "never having cast off completely the accidental and the soluble." I think that by "accidental" the historical is meant; and I join Shaw in being fond of the historical and, especially, the soluble, even if the solutions are difficult. Even when the force of Shaw's dialectics threatens to unhinge the narrative and reason, his plays are rooted deeply in, and filled with, an optimism derived deeply from both narrative (history, the accidental) and reason. Dearly as I love Wilde, I would rather have written *St. Joan* or *Man and Superman* than *The Importance of Being Earnest*.

To write that, to make such comparison, is to commit a grave injustice: Wilde was destroyed at an early age by reactionaries, conservatives, liberals, and homophobes (and I know, I know, you can't call them "homophobes" because there are no "homosexuals" and blah blah blah). Shaw, who outlived Methuselah, produced those masterpieces from a mature genius the time for the ripening of which Wilde was brutally denied. Yeats makes this point, too, in his beautiful introduction to Wilde's *The Happy Prince*. It's interesting that Yeats prefers Wilde's aestheticism to Shaw's socialism, given how clearly Yeats identifies at least one utilitarian aspect of Wilde's purple prose: as calling card to other pre-"homosexual" homosexuals.

> The other day I found at the end of one of [Wilde's] volumes in the section called "Poems in Prose" [from whence comes "The House of Judgment," which ends *Gross Indecency*] such description as "Fair pillars of mar-

ble," "the loud noise of many lutes," "the hall of chalcedony and of jasper," "torches of cedar," "One whose face and raiment were painted and whose feet were shod with pearls." The influence of painting upon English literature which began with the poetry of Keats had now reached its climax, because all educated England was overshadowed by Whistler, by Burne-Jones, by Rossetti; and Wilde—a provincial like myself—found in that influence something of the mystery, something of the excitement, of a religious cult that promised an impossible distinction. It was precisely because he was not of it by birth and by early association that he caught up phrases and adjectives for their own sake, and not because they were a natural part of his design, and spoke them to others as though it were his duty to pass on some password, sign or countersign.

This prose that puts on fancy dress, that does drag, that "poses," this non-naturalness of which Wilde was prime exponent, high priest(ess), this artificiality which calls attention to, which celebrates and indicts the assuming of identity and disguise—surely this is an aspect of homosexual male writing, a feature of our cultural distinctiveness, discernible in Gide, in Genet, in Edmund White, in Dale Peck. It has always driven tough guys nuts, especially tough-guy writers (though I have to say that I have always loved Mailer for his incredible campiness). Poems-in-prose is perversion, a signal to the demimonde. In this as in so much else Oscar was our forefather, or at least the most spectacular shill of the many nineteenth-century radical traditions that combined to produce the human resistance and response to the inhuman onslaught of modernity we call modernism.

Of Wilde as homosexual ur-mother/father so much has

been written. *Gross Indecency*, thrillingly willing to ask its audience to think, comes with its own critical apparatus, at the top of Act Two, as I've mentioned. It's a radical thing these days, asking an audience to contemplate, at a time in history when we're all hot for action (and haven't a clue about direction or purpose or goal). It's so entirely appropriate to use Wilde, theater traditionalist and radical, as the opportunity for trying something new onstage. Moisés Kaufman's play strikes me as something new, for all that he acknowledges his debt to Piscator and Brecht. I'm electrified by the dialectic in *Gross Indecency* between the carnal and the intellectual/historical/political. Look, for instance, at the frightening, funny, sexy scene in which Wilde's erstwhile dinner companions/fuckbuddies betray him and save themselves. To say that, in its mixture of appetite, intelligence, verbal dazzlement, hubris, class conflict, tragedy, and comedy, the play here attains Shakespearean dimensions is not to say that it is old-fashioned; for in this time of caution, modesty, and circumspection-to-the-point-of-trivialization in dramatic writing (policed by certain drama critics), the most genuinely radical playwrights of our time are busy (re)discovering Shakespeare's inexhaustible exuberance.

Wilde's relationship to the stage was always generative. Yeats makes the intriguing point, in the same introduction, that in Wilde's last works his voice is growing less gilded, becoming more "natural," by which Yeats seems to mean less like other writers of his day and more purely itself. This process begins before the trials happen, and Yeats identifies its cause as being a sharpening of Wilde's talents as a playwright, "constrained to that discovery [of his natural voice] by the rigorous techniques of the stage." Playwriting, which so many novelists and poets dismiss, can receive no higher honor than this: that William Butler Yeats believed—and he was right—that writing for the stage brought the best out in Oscar Wilde.

The truth of this observation makes it all the more apt and satisfying that Moisés Kaufman so thoroughly succeeds here in conveying some of the best of Wilde to that rough and exigent realm, and does so without vulgarizing, coarsening, or making less contradictory and maddening this infinitely protean, mutable mind. In the course of *Gross Indecency* the glamor of the earlier prose mainly inhabits what you, the reader of the text, can't see: the exquisitely "off" choices in lighting, the parrot-splendid Huysmans-inflected decor of the production, balanced gaspingly on a tightwire between Edwardian perfection and the slightly appalling beauty, "decadent," which lies just past the threshold of surety and balance. It inhabits the elegant precision of Michael Emerson's magnificent performance, the agony summoned up when his polished magic fails the magician. As you read, you will have to stage it all in the theater in your head, which is the joy of reading a play—but know, those of you who didn't see the staged event for which this work of literature is also the score, that it played every bit as well as you can imagine it would.

I conclude by returning to Mr. Kaufman. As an example of Wilde's fustian prosody gunking up what is pure and beautiful, Yeats cites the first time he heard Wilde's simple, terrifying parable in which Christ re-encounters the people he's cured miraculously, all of whom have since fallen into debauchery and despair. Yeats is unhappy with the story's fancy-dress appearance as "The Doer of Good" in *Poems in Prose*, for it has acquired those pseudo-biblical tones and C. B. DeMille raimentation (the theatrical value of which Kaufman understands perfectly when he positions the similar "House of Judgment" as his play's punch line); the story lacks the "sculptural simplicity" it had when Yeats first heard it. Wilde, he was told, recited this story to himself in the wake of his great string of theatrical successes, suddenly slightly wealthy, acclaimed. . . . Lazarus, whom Christ meets weeping by the roadside, answers, when his Savior asks him why he's lamenting: "Lord, I was dead and you raised me into life, what else can I do but weep?" This is, writes Yeats:

> . . . the melancholy that comes upon a man at the moment of triumph, the only moment when a man without dreading some secret bias, envy, disappointment, jealousy, can ask himself, what is the value of life?

Wilde escaped prolongation of that immanent melancholy by the imminence of the world's grotesque injustice: the jackals and hyenas descended, and Wilde met the Catholic-inflected martyrdom he dreaded and rushed to embrace, heroically self-sacrificing but denied the presumptive certainty that his sacrifice was anything other than vain; in torment to the very last. Here is a play that presents Wilde's passion in all its terrible, tragic force, presents it more intelligently, joyfully, sensually, and politically (which is to say, contradictions flaming) than anything I have ever read or seen on the subject.

And for Mr. Kaufman, and all the contributors to the dazzling success of *Gross Indecency*—all of you children of a better age than the one you've so wonderfully and movingly resurrected, children, too, of a really rotten, unjust, polluted, and impaupered present—good luck with the post-miracle melancholia! Take a tip from Oscar, his indolence and indulgence and his sensuality, and his astonishing industry (for all that he hated the word): there is much to do, after being raised from the dead, besides weeping. Look at the legacy that Wilde's industry has left behind, from which so much has descended, including this beautiful play.